CHRISTOPHER LOWELL'S
ONE-OF-A-KIND
Decorating Projects

CHRISTOPHER LOWELL'S
ONE-OF-A-KIND
Decorating Projects

Fast & Flexible Ways
to Personalize Your Home

Clarkson Potter/Publishers
New York

Photograph on page 5 and illustrations on pages 26, 27, 31 (top left), 66, 67, 100, 110 (right), 123 (top left), 136, 137, and 153 (top left) courtesy of the author; photographs on pages 31 (right, in Variation), 33 (right, in Variation), 55 (top right), 84, 85, 108, 112, 121 (top), 125, 151, and 155 by Douglas Hill; all other photographs by Scott Dunbar Photography.

Arts and Crafts magazine cover used by permission of Krause Publications. Simplicity® Patterns on page 58 (left), 92 (left), 128 (left), and 164 (above and below left) used by permission of Simplicity Pattern Co., Inc.

For more Christopher Lowell ideas and inspirations, log onto
www.christopherlowell.com

Management for Christopher Lowell: Associated Talent Management

Published in the United States by Clarkson Potter/Publishers, an imprint of the Crown Publishing Group, a division of Random House, Inc., New York.
www.crownpublishing.com
www.clarksonpotter.com

Clarkson N. Potter is a trademark and Potter and colophon are registered trademarks of Random House, Inc.

Library of Congress Cataloging-in-Publication Data
Lowell, Christopher.
Christopher Lowell's one-of-a-kind decorating projects : fast & flexible ways to personalize your home / Christopher Lowell.
1. Handicraft.   2. House furnishings.   3. Interior decoration.
I. Title.
II. Title: One-of-a-kind decorating projects.
TT157.L68   2007
747—dc22   2006015191

ISBN 978-0-307-34171-6

Printed in Japan

Design by Caitlin Daniels Israel

10 9 8 7 6 5 4 3 2 1

First Edition

DEDICATION

This book is dedicated to my amazing brother, Jeff. While in many ways we could not be more different, we did share something profound in common: a bedroom. To this day I'm convinced that Neil Simon based *The Odd Couple* on us. A guy's guy who would just as soon deck you as discuss a point, Jeff had to put up with artsy-fartsy me always rearranging the furniture. He would invariably stumble over a chair in the dark while trying to sneak in after curfew, and I would wake up to him screaming at me, "What the [insert favorite cuss word here]!" It wasn't pretty. But boy, my room sure was. I say "mine" because that's what ended up happening as a result of our deal. Early on, in our bedroom in San Diego, I'd taken a very large red corduroy bedspread and hung it from the ceiling with thumbtacks, thereby dividing the room rightfully, I thought, in half. At least that's how it started. Every time Jeff came in late or committed some other infraction and didn't want me to "tell" (thus risking Dad's impressive wrath), I'd move the red wall an inch farther into his side. That wall was my hush money. Suffice it to say, Jeff was a bad, bad boy. Jeff was always late, late, late. Jeff was always in trouble, trouble, trouble. See Jeff lose his side of the room. Bye-bye, room! In less than a year, my red curtain had reached the side of Jeff's twin bed, which was, you guessed it, against the wall. Poor Jeff actually had to crawl over the footboard to get into it. God bless him, he kept to the terms. The "Don't ask, don't tell" policy worked well for many years.

While Jeff could be a hothead, he was also my protector. Under all that machismo, my brother was and is one of the most tender hearts I've known. Let someone mess with his creepy, nerdy, verbose kid brother, who wore his sweater tucked into his too-high pants, played the piano, spouted Shakespeare, and decorated . . . well, you could lose an eye! Years later when I watched the movie *Stand By Me,* I got a lump in my throat. River Phoenix's character, Chris Chambers, was my brother, Jeff. Today, he sleeps well in his own room some three thousand miles away in Florida, and he's still defending my right to be me. See you in clown alley, buddy. (Only he'll know what that means.)

CONTENTS

PREFACE 9

INTRODUCTION 11

TOWN: LOFTY IDEAS 21

Town Desk 30

Spin City: The Lazy Swivel Storage Unit 34

Pipe-Dream Coffee Table 36

Sand-sational Cactus Garden 38

A-Head of the Rest 44

It's a Stretch! Art on a Budget 48

Ottomatic, Automatic 52

COUNTRY: OPEN TO THE PUBLIC: SHARED SPACES 61

Bolster Your Room's Ego 72

Marbleizing 79

Paint Abuse: Distressing 82

Vases on the Ropes 90

CONCLUSION 167

RESOURCES 168

CONTACT INFORMATION 171

ACKNOWLEDGMENTS 172

INDEX 173

CITY: SEXY SPACES: MASTERING THE MASTER 95

A Window's Royal Crown 106

Heavenly Headboard 110

A Platform for Creativity: Zen Bed 114

Bamb-beautiful Vases 118

SHORE: SPACE: THE FINAL FRONT HALL 131

Beachcomber's Corner: Framing Nature 144

Hideaway Desk: A Two Bookcase Study 152

Made in the Shade:
Super-Simple Lamp Shade 156

Light the Way 160

Oh, What a Relief It Is: Easy 3-D Stenciling 162

PREFACE

During an entire summer of my childhood, I could not wait to return home from Bible camp. Though set in the beautiful New Hampshire mountains, this religious penitentiary of mandatory "crafting" drove me into prepubescent insanity. I remember the comb case I had to make: two fake leather pieces sewn together with a black plastic shoelace thingy—are you kidding me here? First of all, I had a crew cut . . . why did I need a comb, much less a case for it? And why, if it took us two excruciating hours to drive up those mountains (which were begging to be explored), were we forced to sit inside and make log cabins out of Popsicle sticks? I felt duped—creatively frustrated and unsatisfied.

Thereafter, anyone who even mentioned the word "craft" to me would unwittingly send me back to that summer when I realized that fussy, cutesy crafts for therapy were *not* on my agenda. They weren't then, and thirty years later they still aren't.

It wasn't until 1994, when I opened the doors of Christopher Lowell's Decorative Home Arts Center in Chagrin Falls, Ohio, that the "c" word turned up again like a bad penny. At that time, our research told us that to the modern working woman, the word "craft" meant something her child did in preschool or her grandmother did in the rest home. To multitasking moms and put-upon professional women, crafts were done by people with way too much time on their hands.

So since the last thing *I* wanted to be guilty of was making people feel as if they were at Bible camp, I instead taught interior design, faux finishes, tablescaping, home entertaining, and so forth. But never crafting! My strategy worked, and it was obvious that the women who signed up for my courses were an entirely different breed from those who went to the crafting, quilting, and needlepoint classes just a few doors down.

These busy women—my students—just didn't have a lot of use for macramé toilet-paper-roll covers. But giving a beaten-up old end table new life with a bit of marbleizing? You betcha. Creating a cushy ottoman to provide extra seating *and* hidden storage? Yessiree. Are you starting to see the difference? You will . . . you . . . will.

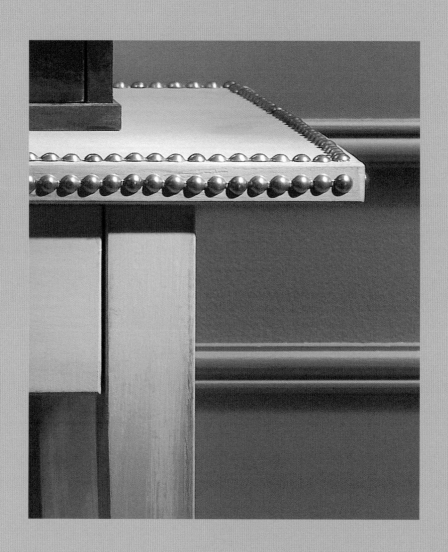

INTRODUCTION

WHAT'S SO GREAT ABOUT "CUSTOM"?

What's so great about custom interior design? Well, frankly, everything. What isn't great about having exactly what you want, where and how you want it, and exactly to your taste and specifications? It's why couture fits better than Kmart; why Mom's cooking tastes better than McDonald's (at least my mom's did); and why a room with made-to-order cabinetry and specially upholstered furniture probably looks better than one with all store-bought, ready-made items. "Better"—that is, unless we are resourceful and a little bit clever. Because while we cannot deny that custom design is often well worth its effort, we also cannot deny the price. Ouch. Custom costs.

Let me explain. As I'm sure you have discovered, the minute you step foot over the line from ready-made into the world of "custom," prices immediately double and often triple. And in the world of interior design, "custom," to a lot of decorators (*ka-ching*), means "pay dirt."

But hey! I've spent a good part of my career figuring out—and teaching—fun and practical ways around those high costs of money and of time, and I thought putting those ideas into a book for my readers and viewers seemed like a good idea. So here it is. Whether what you need right now is down-to-earth and practical or indulgent and decorative, chances are you will find it here in these pages. And if you don't find the exact item of your heart's desire, you'll find an item or an idea close enough to it to send you on your own creative way. We show you everything from a desk storage unit, to a recycled countertop, to a versatile ottoman, to a good-looking vase, and more.

Our mission is to create for you an inventory of skills—decorators' tricks, really—that will enable you to customize your house using mass-market materials and midtier retailers without the need for a professional designer and an expensive custom workroom.

Here's the deal: With a bit of tweaking, those ready-made curtains from Kmart could *look* custom if you added a lining and maybe some fringe or a border. Finished curtains from Pottery Barn may already be lined but not long enough or decorative enough for your needs. By adding fringe and a wide fabric border to match your interior, you actually have created a custom look. You may also see a bookshelf displayed in

a store in a conventional way. But turn the shelves on their side unconventionally (as you'll see us do in this book), and it becomes a support base and an altogether different and custom thing.

It's this adding-to and adapting business that this book is all about. Suddenly, with a little augmenting and reinterpreting, a store-bought piece becomes one of a kind and custom, and no one is the wiser—or poorer! Most of these projects can be done in less than a day, including your time spent shopping and preparing. This is called embellishing, not crafting. We are enhancing through decoration, not creating art. Get it? Good.

Since everything in our finished rooms comes from national chain stores, you should be able to find most everything in or near your own town or city. By using the resource guide at the back of this book, you can also order a product online knowing that we've already seen it in person, worked with it, and given it our seal of approval. That's cool, right?

If you want a refresher on interior design, my book *Christopher Lowell's Seven Layers of Design* is good for that, and the rest of my books will help you to determine your own style. This book is about customizing your home for a look that is all about you.

Still wondering if you are the "crafty" type? I hear you, sister; read on. . . .

CONFLICTED ABOUT CRAFTING?

Are you? Conflicted about crafting, I mean? I certainly was not, as you read in the Preface, but it made things a little tricky from a practical, semantic standpoint. The craft embargo I'd begun in the nineties was staunchly maintained from that point on. And as I began to develop my first television series, one of the show's strictest rules was to never, under any circumstances, mention the words "craft" or "hobby." "Project" was fine; "craft," *never*.

This was no easy feat since professional crafters made up a significant number of our show's guests. Try getting through an eight-minute TV segment with a hard-core crafter without ever mentioning the word "craft." But somehow I managed this tap dance and no one was the wiser. Over the next seven years, many of the nation's top crafters graced our studios, and I wound up on the front cover of *Arts and Crafts* magazine. Go figure. Talk about feeling conflicted. . . . Just what was it about the idea of crafting that I seemed either to resent or just not get?

I began to really listen to the crafters who came on my show. When I asked them why they crafted, they said it was as much about the process as it was about the result. They said they could become so absorbed in what they were doing that time would either stand still or fly by. Aha, there it was . . . that time thing again—time and patience. Well, bingo—I have never had much of either.

I grew up with ADD, dyslexic, and poor, often working several jobs at once. So even if I wanted to, the experience of "crafting for escape" escaped me. While I always made things and was good with my hands, I created things because I needed them. It was a way to

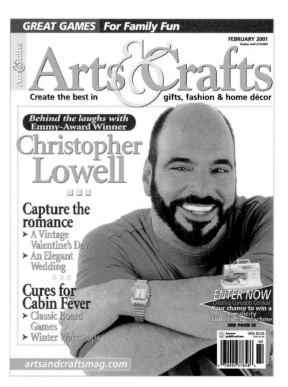

save money. If I didn't construct it, I wouldn't have it. Simple as that. I didn't design things to pass time, and I guess deep down, I must have resented people who had time to spare.

My main requirement was that each project had to be functional. It had to be more than cute and endearing. This became the very mandate for any demonstration I allowed on my show. It had to be fun and creative, *and* it had to be practical. The result had to be worth the time, money, and effort expended. So there it was in its little decoupage nutshell: I was just way too pragmatic to be a crafter. For great art, I would suffer; for a pot rack, I would not, and I am both an exhibiting artist and an interior designer.

That is not to say decoration or design cannot be artful or artistic, because it can. It is just not worth suf-

fering for. What I am saying here, people, is you do not have to be an artist to use this book. Your desire for a beautiful and well-functioning home, plus a little enthusiasm and a bit of elbow grease, is all you need.

HOW TO USE THIS BOOK

We find that when we ask many people what their preferred style is, they are uncertain. Some still think that "Chippendale" refers to a male strip club and not the eighteenth-century furniture designer. But when we ask, "If budget were no object, where would you like to live? Are you a town, country, city, or shore person?" most people know the answer immediately. A mental image springs to mind. And as soon as people make that determination, it automatically dictates a theme they might be comfortable living with. That's why we organized the book by four specific lifestyles: Town, Country, City, and Shore. In fact, these are the same four lifestyle categories in which my company designs all our retail furnishings.

Each of these lifestyle groups allows a wide range of interpretation. For example, *Town* can be a modern eclectic look with warm woods and a layering of great textures, which is the case in our interpretation in this book. But it might also reflect old-world manor-house style. A sense of timeless order allows formal antiques to live happily with modern and even high-tech touches for a feeling of relaxed luxury.

Country can be interpreted as an update on the classic American look of Shaker furniture, braided rugs, primitive art, and homespun fabrics. Or it can be interpreted as European country, where fine art and furnishings live side by side with primitive pieces and handcrafted keepsakes, and play off vibrant color. It, too, is eclectic. A piece of formal silver might be placed on a sideboard next to a carved wooden bowl. Our Country look is warm and charming; it has the comfortable feeling of a bed-and-breakfast, but with a fresh, chic attitude.

City brings us sleek, pared-down sophistication with an uncluttered, uptown point of view. It's the most intentional look, where all decorating choices are deliberate. The tranquil feeling of East meets West is perfect for this cool, modern, and orderly urban mix.

Shore—ahhhh. The coastal dream of endless beaches and windswept dunes. Clean lines and sun-bleached colors will transport you to a seafarer's paradise.

Each of our four finished rooms represents one of these lifestyles. As you examine the

projects, remember that Town, Country, City, and Shore are simply launching points for your creative imagination. And every one of these lifestyles can be interpreted in a variety of ways. For instance, Shore could mean "Nantucket Americana" with the addition of stenciling to a pillow cushion. The same project could easily be tweaked with the addition of an appliqué or a tassel to reflect, say, "Isle of Capri." Both are Shore concepts but interpreted in very different ways; the point I'm making here is that the categories are not to limit you but to give you a framework of ideas. That's why I'll often give you suggestions for minor style variations to help you visualize how to fit these projects into your décor. It is up to you to customize as you desire.

Speaking of which, when you view our projects and our finished rooms, don't just look at their style. Look *past* the decoration and theme of the room for ideas that will work for you. For example, you may not want the "Zen" look of our City room, but the way we arranged the furniture or the lighting might be perfect for your home. Observe how we've used space, faux finishes, fabric, mirrors, color, light, scale . . . it all adds up. You may pull a bookcase idea from one room and a storage idea from another. These simple concepts will help you draw together a room for a custom look that *will* rock your world.

PEP TALK

Got your pom-poms ready?
Good! Let's go!

TWO-FOUR-SIXTY-ONE,
THE PROJECTS HERE ARE FUN, FUN, FUN!

All right, all right. I just want to emphasize that the projects in this book are to inspire you and to help you get your house together on a reasonable budget and time line, with professional-looking results. I know you may not be an artist, but you are creative.

Personal creativity is innate. It is like breathing. We exhibit this pure creativity all day long. It's just that we take it for granted. As I always say, if you can get up, get dressed, put on makeup, do your hair, and drive in busy traffic, you are already overqualified to do the tasks in this book.

Some of the projects we show you are to make from scratch. Some you'll find ready-made: Buy and assemble and you're good to go. Still other items show ordinary ready-made things being used in extraordinary ways. Of course you are always free to embellish our projects in any way you see fit. Go for it.

There isn't one thing in this book that anyone cannot do. We've worked hard to make sure of that. It's up to you to stay positive and enthusiastic and to keep your sense of humor. I know you can do it.

THE TEN (CREATIVITY) COMMANDMENTS

Okay, "commandment" may be a little strong, but I promise, you will be a lot better off if you consider these ten tips before beginning almost any creative project. And especially for our purposes here, keep in mind that we are *customizing,* not *crafting.* But regardless of what you call it, anytime you can bring a mental vision into three dimensions, you have done something very powerful. So naturally, your frame of mind is all important. Each time you tap into your own creative spirit, you prove to yourself that you can do it, and you give your soul a gift. Our personal creativity was given to us as an antidote to stress, so isn't it time we started to enjoy it?

1 Before you begin, focus on the result, and decide to enjoy getting there. Don't focus on what you can't do because you've never done it before. And don't let your lack of experience keep you from doing a project. What, you're going to let a little ol' paintbrush make you afraid? Come on now . . .

2 Lighten up, already! Make fun a prerequisite. No Christopher Lowell book would be complete without the following statement: *Where there is fear, there is no creativity.* You make hundreds of creative decisions a day; it is just that over time those decisions have become automatic to you. Remember: We learn by doing and we perfect what we do by repeating it. When we do something successfully, our self-esteem increases and we feel positive and less fearful.

3 Grant yourself permission to do a project, and seek your permission alone. We sometimes become insecure and may subconsciously look for someone else to sabotage us by talking us out of the project. We might run into someone who we know is going to be skeptical, either of what we are undertaking or of our ability to complete it. Save yourself the aggravation and the downer, and avoid those kinds of people or keep your project plans to yourself. On the other hand, if you know someone who will support you, enroll him or her as a partner.

4 Think the project through, step-by-step. Or, as they used to say in grade school, read the directions all the way through before beginning. I know, roll your eyes and say duh, but you'd be surprised at how people set themselves up for failure because they look at a photo and think, "Piece of cake." Read carefully. Be absolutely clear on the steps required and the kind of space you need to do them in. If you're painting six separate elements, where do they go when they're drying? Know what comes next. It's hard to turn a page if both your hands are covered in glue. By having a mental picture of how the project will progress, you heighten your prospects for success.

5 Adapt, adjust, execute. If you are going to customize a project (and you should!), make those decisions before you begin and decide how you will need to adjust the original instructions. How long, high, or wide do you want the item to be? How do you want it to perform? Where will you put it when it's done? What color do you want it to be? Are there mechanical considerations of construction or support? For example, if we show you an easy roll-away table that measures 4 feet and you want one that's 8 feet, chances are you'll need to devise stronger center support, right?

6 Let the need for the project propel you forward. For those of you (like me) who fear wasting time on anything frivolous, clarify what need or desire the project fulfills for you and the priority you place on that fulfillment. If the idea is to make something you really want for a fraction of the store-bought cost, then it is worth the investment of your time. More important, it is an opportunity to train your creative eye and learn a new skill.

7 Find a creative space. Designate an area that can be devoted to doing your project from beginning to end. Nothing will snuff out the creative spark more quickly than repeatedly having to set up and break down your tools and materials. Make room in your schedule, too, before you begin. Don't give yourself unrealistic deadlines that could stress you and take the fun out of the creative process.

8 Do trial runs. Don't be afraid to practice, test, or experiment first. If it's a painting technique you've never done before, try it on a scrap of something until you feel comfortable with it, before moving on to the real project. Nothing's worse than having a project 90 percent done and then botching the whole thing because of one goof.

9 Gather the right tools. They'll make all the difference. A low-temperature glue gun is different from a high-temperature one. An upholstery needle is different from a knitting needle. If the job requires a specific knife, don't think a really sharp pair of scissors will do. While I invite you to be inventive, I don't mean with tools. If one of our projects requires a hammer, don't just substitute the little stocking stuffer one with the pink handle you got at Christmas. We mean a regular, full-size one for grown-ups. You can sometimes substitute materials, but don't skimp on good tools. They are a worthy investment, and if you take care of them, you'll have them for a long time.

10 Ask questions. If you're not sure about something, don't be afraid to ask, and for heaven's sake, don't be embarrassed. Whether at your local hardware store or craft store, you'll find that people love to help, give advice, and just plain show off what they know. And there is always the Internet.

AND JUST FOR GOOD MEASURE . . .

You know I don't usually talk about taste, but . . . the art of restraint will always serve you well. "Less is best." When in doubt, do less, and don't be afraid to edit if you overdo it. It is all part of the creative process. If something starts to look tacky, it is because you are trying too hard or didn't follow directions. Shortcuts usually don't work. If you're gonna do it, do it right! Half the thrill is taking the bow for what you have accomplished. And you can't do that when you have to make excuses for the outcome, right? Okay—'nuf said!

Now get going! You can do it!

LOFTY IDEAS

Over the years I've received literally thousands of requests for what we call one-room living ideas and solutions. These are for the spatially deprived who have only one open space to live in. Creating various areas for various tasks is key not only to staying organized but also to keeping your sanity. The idea here is to divide the space into rooms within rooms. That way you have some place else to go . . . dig?

On a small budget, with no carpenter and a persnickety landlord, many people find the prospect of reconfiguring an interior space daunting, and therefore do nothing. Thus their spaces look like dorm rooms rather than the sophisticated loftlike or studio environments they could be. Such is the case with this room. Having been purged of its junk, it's ready for its makeover. Look closely. What is there isn't bad at all. The ready-to-assemble bookcases seem to be in good shape. So, let's save some money and use what we've got. The fact that they're black will make that color an obvious accent in the finished room's overall scheme. What is not working is where they are placed. While it is certainly okay to line a wall with bookcases, wall space here is at a premium. And do we want to see everything in the bookcases from everywhere in the room? Some of it is

attractive, but some items might be better hidden in closed decorative storage.

The neutral sofa opposite the bookcases is rather nice and in excellent condition. But facing a food cooler supporting the TV? I think we can do better than that. The sofa seems to be taking up most of the center of the room when it need not, and it has a direct view of the bed. Creating privacy by actually making a separate bedroom area will help this space function so much better. Here the bed is shoved into a corner, making it accessible on only one side. Hard to share it (I won't go there) and hard to make it up each morning. Wouldn't it be nice to lie in bed and actually look out the window? Yes, that is a window, but the two chests of drawers block half of it. Gridlock!

Separating the bed, the chests, and the bookcases into at least three nice focal points could ease this furniture jam. The chests are necessary for storage but could use some dressing up. Perhaps a paint job and embellishing might help. The drafting board/desk could also be minimized or even eliminated if a proper work area was built into the space.

UNCLUTTER ME BEAUTIFUL

Clutter is a killer in the creative process. Before we began decorating any room, we purged it, following the steps set forth in my book *Christopher Lowell's Seven Layers of Organization*. In it I outline a comprehensive system for streamlining and reorganizing the home in about ten days. And what is really important is how we examine this process from an emotional and psychological point of view. If getting rid of junk was just a matter of throwing it away, there wouldn't be a cluttered home in America, would there?

So if you think part of your decorating problem is that you really need to clear out your junk and clutter, then grab the bull by the horns and do it. No sense making decorative items for rooms that already have too much in them or that frankly don't function the way you'd really like them to.

On a budget, repurposing is key. Watch how much of what you see shows up in our finished room.

"Let texture tell your story."

1 COLOR PALETTE

Monochromatic, ranging from deep tan to chocolate brown. A color scheme like this is ideal for a unisex look because it is gender neutral. It's also great for the beginner who might feel insecure about mixing and matching a lot of different colors and patterns.

The walls are painted Walnut Shell and the trim Arrowroot; both are from the Christopher Lowell Designer Paint line. The wall color is dark enough to be warm and enveloping but not so dark as to be oppressive. The subtle color contrast between the walls and the bookcases creates a harmony.

2 TEXTURE

After the shell of the room has been painted, it's all about layering interesting textures, fabrics, and materials within the monochromatic color palette.

Light cocoa chenille and woven tweed will be ideal for bed coverings and high-ticket upholstery such as the sofa.

Cream-colored quilted poly-silk for bed pillow accents will add a textured geometric element without introducing another pattern.

The fun, chic faux poodle fur contributes a dense texture to the room but should be used sparingly on items such as bed throws or ottoman covers. This assures that it remains classic and not faddish.

3 ORGANIC ELEMENTS

The reed-bamboo window treatments bring a hint of Asian flair to our room. Their natural, organic vibe will be a springboard for other accessories that can weave this element evenly throughout the room.

Translucent sheers with embedded pinstripes will soften the room both acoustically and visually. Layered against our walnut-colored walls, the material will add yet another subtle geometric element to the mix.

4 ACCENTS

High-tech elements like flange and pipe, silver, chrome, polished tin, and wire mesh will act as metallic accents, or the room's jewelry. Spread evenly around the room, these accents will provide sparkle and a hip attitude against the moody background.

Look at your rooms from fresh perspectives. We get used to seeing the same things in the same rooms, and we forget we're the people who put the stuff there in the first place. So it is perfectly okay for us to change our minds and remove or alter whatever isn't working anymore.

To do this, ask yourself, If money were no object, how would I like this space to work? Chances are you would simply like an attractive, functional space. How extravagant is that? It isn't the expense; it's the ingenuity. So get that creative cap on and dream a little. Or a lot. Any of my books, including this one, will help you do just that. You *can* do it.

It is always a good idea to work out everything on paper first. The simplest digital cameras allow us to photograph and print images with ease. Take a photo of your existing or emptied room, and place a clear acetate sheet on top of it. Sketch out possible furniture plans and window treatments with a felt marker. Don't be afraid to refine until you get it the way you want it.

This is an invaluable guide and reference point to keep you on track and positive, and in the long run you'll save money and time. Cool, huh?

With the room empty, we have a clean slate and can begin to see just how substantial this space really is. Dividing space doesn't necessarily mean putting up walls. For example, if configured differently, the bookcases could actually create a bedroom area or at least a surround, which would offer privacy and solve storage problems. How? Just because bookcases are made to go against the wall doesn't mean they have to . . . hint, hint! Of course the real goal is to see if we can block the bed from the other living spaces altogether.

To warm up the space, wall color could do wonders. Keeping the color neutral will add a sense of sophistication. Taking our cue from the sofa, we will use various tones from deep putty to light beige, with black accents (established by the bookcases), to make this room unisex and chic. And since we're doing a lot of beige on beige, we might want to think in terms of layering. I want to explore the idea of using simple artists' canvas stretchers covered with sheer fabric, and simply hung as is. Acoustically the covered frames will muffle bedroom and living room noise; artistically they will be a subtle and attractive arrangement. When it all comes together, the space will be dramatically transformed and one of a kind. Custom looks without custom buck$. Love that!

FROM DOWNTOWN TO UPTOWN

Rather than thinking of this space as a simple studio apartment, we chose to think of it as a great hotel suite. And as with any superb-quality hotel, there are traditional elements of luxury and comfort, considerate touches that are familiar and welcoming—a good thing for a hotel, right? Hotel designers understand this, and now you do, too. Translating this to the home is simple; we'll aim to include all the amenities you'd

expect from a five-star hotel and a look that is gender neutral so anyone who occupies it will feel at home. As we think about the future of young multitasking couples participating together in all decisions about their home, creating a look that accommodates both their tastes will be key.

This room proves that it is never about size; it is about your ability to think outside the box (even if a box is the only thing you've got to work with). The bed, once pushed against the wall and in full view of the entire studio, has been enclosed by the same six bookcases that were already in the room. The effect is to divide the studio into two well-defined spaces, with the bed area now relatively private and the living area distinct.

Here's how we did it: To make the bed surround, we positioned two bookcases side by side close to the halfway point in the center of the room. We screwed the bookcases together where the sides touch and turned them to face the new living room area. Beside

those we positioned pairs of back-to-back bookcases, so that one side faces the side of the bed—for instant bedside tables—and the other side faces out toward the room.

The unfinished back of the side-by-side bookcases was upholstered to function as a headboard in the new bedroom. This is shown on page 44. When the bed is made up, the look is luxurious enough for her yet tailored enough for him.

On the bedroom side of each bookcase, to give the illusion of openness and space, we added mirror panels at about the level of the top of the bed. The rest of the bedroom-side shelves are used for things like the alarm clock, reading material, a secretary for letter writing, remote controls, and a telephone.

On the living room side of the bookcases we created an efficient and eye-catching workstation and storage area with nothing more than fiberboard and flanges.

In short order, without the need for a carpenter or a mortgage broker, these bookcases have completely redefined the spaces, adding significant architectural interest, storage, privacy, and even a generous workstation.

BEEN HERE? DONE THIS?

Throughout this studio (and the whole book, in fact) we've given examples of how storage containers can not only hide your stash but also become part of the room's design. Use open storage for things you don't mind seeing, closed storage for stuff you want hidden. Today the textures and surfaces of storage containers will integrate into almost any environment. As our look here is modern with a touch of Zen, we found that wicker, reed, and leather containers mixed well with chrome, tin, and wire mesh to give us the attitude we were looking for.

TOWN DESK

In small spaces like studio apartments, every inch *has* to count. We built this workstation off the bookcases facing the living room area. The backs of the bookcases have been padded as a headboard for a bed surround (see page 44). While we used this configuration in the center of a space, you can easily adapt it to any place that can fit two ready-to-assemble bookcases (from your local office supply store) side by side.

This project, including shopping, should take about a day.

(see page 44)

MATERIALS AND TOOLS

2 ready-to-assemble bookcases

1 sheet of 1/2-inch MDF (medium-density fiberboard)

Tape measure

Pencil

Jigsaw

Trim

Sandpaper

Caulking primer

Wood paint

Standard pipes (make sure to have the store thread them to your measurements)

4 flanges

Screws

Drill

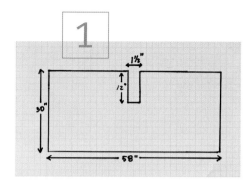

1

1 After assembling your two identical bookcases, place them side by side. Your goal is to establish the measurement for a desktop, which you'll make from MDF (medium-density fiberboard). Measure the combined interior width of the two bookcases (in our case it was 58 inches). Measure the shelf depth and determine how far you want the desktop to protrude into the room (in our case it was 30 inches). This will give you the total dimensions of your desktop.

• Where the bookcases meet in the center, measure the total thickness of the two sides. Then measure the depth of the bookshelf. This will give you the dimensions of the notch you'll have to cut out so you can slip the desktop in flush with the back walls of both bookcases resting on the adjustable shelves positioned at desk height (in our case it was 1^1/$_2$ by 12 inches). After drawing the notch onto the center back of your MDF, cut it out with a jigsaw.

2 Finish the desk by adding trim around the edge, sanding, caulking, priming, and painting.

2

To support the desk in the front, create legs with two pipes fitted with flanges at both ends. Our measurement happened to be 27 inches. We took the measurement from the bottom of the desk to the floor and subtracted 3 inches for the connections. Pipes will be available in the plumbing section of your local hardware store.

• Turn the desktop over (facedown) and attach the top flanges to the bottom side of the desktop with screws. Attach two more flanges, one to the bottom of each pipe, to create the feet. When the desktop is in place, these will simply rest on the floor.

3 Slide your finished desktop and pipe-legged unit into the two shelves. And you're good to go!

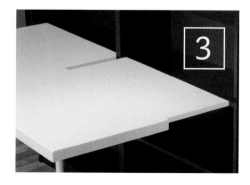

3

V

VARIATION

An instant work center can be created by placing two bookcases, facing out, on either side of an existing table.

To snazz it up a little, we cut bead board the width of the backs of the bookcases and the length of the table, then attached it with finishing nails.

To complete the look, we screwed a hollow-core door into place on top of the bookcases, trimmed it with molding, and mounted two lights to the underside.

GRAND ILLUSIONS

Nothing can visually expand a space better than mirrors. And to prove there really is power in numbers, here, against a deep walnut-colored wall, we hung a dozen identical, wood-framed mirrors. We then spray-painted eight battery-powered picture lights matte silver and fixed them along the top and bottom rows of mirrors, with the lights shining toward one another. Because there are no cords to deal with, they install on walls without electrical outlets. Cool! Not only do the wood frames add architectural interest to the space, but the mirrors inside them reflect an image of the entire room, giving the illusion of yet another groovy space beyond. At night these picture lights and the additional ones we installed on the top of the bookcase/desk area create an ambient glow that's tranquil and sexy.

VARIATION

For a one-of-a-kind mirror, cut out the center of a polyurethane architectural ceiling medallion with a saw and attach a mirror using mirror mastic or mirror clips. Paint or stain as you desire.

Here we used a mirror as a design element over the fireplace.

And here it works as a focal point in the powder room.

SPIN CITY:
THE LAZY SWIVEL STORAGE UNIT

We made this nifty dual-function TV storage tower from three store-bought wooden cubes and lazy Susans. Stacked on top of one another, the cubes are joined by heavy-duty lazy-Susan (turntable) mechanisms from the local hardware store. This allows them to swivel independently and in any direction. It makes for easy TV viewing anywhere in the room while providing additional storage for tapes and DVDs. When not in use, this unit can be turned to act as a stylish mirror tower reflecting all the other cool things in the room. The options are endless and the project is so simple.

This project, including shopping, should take about half a day.

MATERIALS AND TOOLS

Tape measure	Drill
Jigsaw	Screws
½ sheet of ¾ inch MDF (medium-density fiberboard)	Paint (for wood and metal)
Two 12-inch lazy Susan units	3 ready-to-assemble storage cubes

1 Using a jigsaw, cut two 15-inch-diameter circles out of MDF. Cut a 9-inch-diameter circle out of the center of each circle. Screw the lazy-Susan unit to this MDF "doughnut" through its predrilled holes. Repeat with the second "doughnut" and lazy-Susan unit.

2 Paint the unit the color of your wood storage units.

3 Assemble the storage cubes. Screw the metal half of one lazy Susan to the bottom of a storage cube.

4 Place a second storage cube upside down on top of that and screw it to the wood half of the lazy Susan unit. Stack a second lazy Susan unit and a third storage cube and screw them together. With another person, flip the whole thing right side up. (Now you will not see the screws.)

TO ADD MIRROR MAGIC

The unit's top two cubes can freely rotate. To dress up the sides of each cube, we simply screwed three identical mirrors directly into the wood. You could also attach them using mirror mastic. When the mirrors face out into the room, they reflect everything around it. Cool, right?

PIPE-DREAM COFFEE TABLE

Saving money and getting a custom look requires being clever. This easy-to-assemble coffee table required a quick trip to the plumbing section of the local hardware store for pipes, flanges, and felt pads, a stop at one of the "superstores" or an unfinished furniture store for a storage cube (see more cube ideas on page 52), and a ready-cut round glass top. The pipes and flanges can be painted or left as is. Chrome offers a high-tech look, black is sleek and sophisticated, and a primary accent color might give your room just the little "pop" it needs. If you need to clean up the pipes a bit, steel wool will do the trick.

This project, including shopping, should take about half a day.

MATERIALS AND TOOLS

Spray paint for metal, if desired	Screws
	Drill
4 prethreaded 1³⁄₄-inch-long pipes	Peel-and-stick felt pads
8 flanges to fit pipes	1 ready-cut round glass tabletop
1 ready-to-assemble storage cube	

1 If you like, spray-paint the pipes and flanges.

Assemble the cube per the manufacturer's instructions.

2 Now screw four of the flanges into the corners of the cube. Screw the pipes into the attached flanges, and screw the remaining flanges onto those, flat side up.

3 Place the peel-and-stick felt pads at the center of each flange. Place the ready-cut glass on top of the padded flanges.

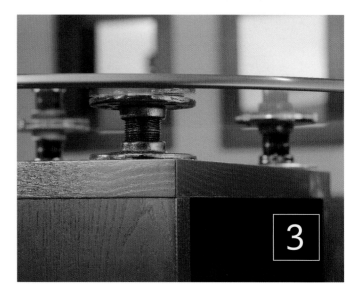

If you want taller cubes to use as side tables, use longer pipe. You could even push two units together and use a ready-cut square or rectangular glass top as a sideboard.

SAND-SATIONAL CACTUS GARDEN

It's the little touches that mean a lot in the overall effect of a finished room. If you're a plant killer like me, you stand a better chance using cacti and succulents. They're abuse-proof! While you can grow cactus in any container, here's a cool option that's just a tad more chic. Be sure to ask for planting soil specifically for cacti and succulents.

This project, including shopping, should take just a few hours. If you already have everything, it should take about as long as a commercial break. It's that easy!

1 From your local nursery or plant store, select a few cacti or succulent plants that you think will cluster well together and add a sense of living architecture to your room. They should be in pots small enough to fit inside glass cylinders of various heights that can be grouped together in odd numbers. (We used three.)

2 From the hobby store, purchase cylinder-shaped Styrofoam to fit inside the cylinder vases. Its diameter should be at least 1 inch smaller than the diameter of the container.

3 Measure the depth of your cactus pot and subtract that plus 1 inch from the height of the cylinder. This measurement will accommodate the depth of the pot without causing the sand to overflow the cylinder. Using a knife, cut the Styrofoam to that length.

4 Place the Styrofoam into the container. With one hand, hold the foam to keep it upright while using the other hand to scoop the sand into the cylinder until it reaches the top of the Styrofoam. Place the potted cactus on top of the Styrofoam and carefully pour the rest of the sand up over the Styrofoam cylinder, letting it overflow into the pot so it looks like the cactus is growing right out of the sand.

CHEAP TCHOTCHKE

Decorative accessories can be easy and cheap without looking like it. Here we attached an ordinary store-bought wooden salad bowl to an unfinished pine plaque and, after priming, spray-painted the whole thing glossy brown. Three metal curtain finials are screwed into the base of the plaque to raise it up a notch. Dried artichokes sprayed with silver paint complete the modern look.

VISUAL BRIDGES

The sides of the bookcase provide great display opportunities. Try a set of framed prints or a mirror or two.

Even these clothes hooks help bridge one bookcase to the other while adding support.

"Layering monochromatic textures can create a look that's classic and timeless."

BEFORE

A-HEAD OF THE REST

Four pieces of ¼-inch plywood, 1-inch foam, and fabric create a stunning headboard while disguising the unfinished backs of two bookcases. Alternatively, this headboard can be mounted directly to the wall (see page 72).

This project, including shopping, should take about half a day.

MATERIALS AND TOOLS

Tape measure	Batting
Jigsaw	Fabric
1 sheet of luan (¼-inch plywood)	Staple gun and staples
Scissors	Industrial-strength Velcro (available at larger hardware centers)
1-inch foam	
Spray adhesive	

1 Measure and use a jigsaw to cut four pieces of luan (or have the hardware store do it) to be placed horizontally across the bookcases. Cut four 1-inch foam pieces the same size as the luan pieces. Using spray adhesive, attach the foam pieces to the luan pieces. Cut a piece of batting the same size as each foam-and-luan segment. Apply a light coat of spray adhesive to the batting. Cover the luan and foam with batting, folding the batting over the edges. Repeat with each panel.

2 Cut the fabric (we used Ultrasuede) 3 inches larger than the panel so you have enough to cover the panel and comfortably fold the fabric around the panel edges, and staple on the backside of the luan, trimming away the excess at the corners. Repeat for each panel.

3 Attach industrial-strength Velcro to the backs of the upholstered panels and bookcases, and attach the panels to the bookcases. (*Tip:* Even though industrial-strength Velcro is extra strong and sticky, you can reinforce it by stapling both sides to the surfaces they are attached to.)

VISUAL BRIDGES

A sexy dual-function head-board provides comfort and drama while also finishing off the raw backs of two side by side bookcases.

MITERED CORNERS— ADDING ON TO A DUVET

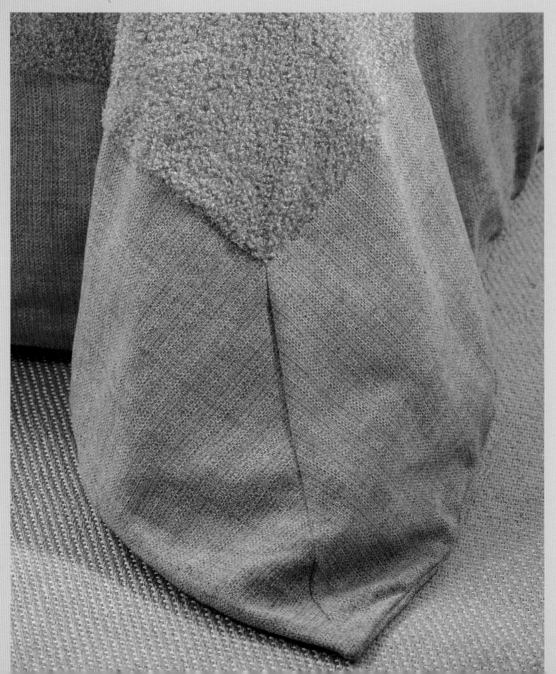

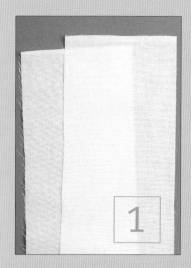

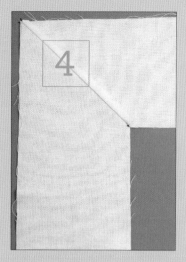

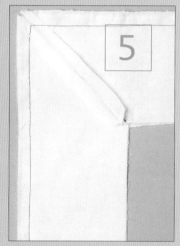

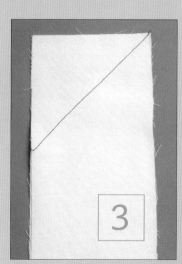

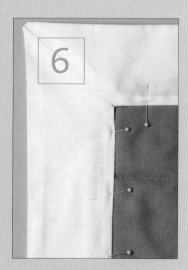

You know what you like, so go buy your fabrics and add this designer detail. If you can sew a straight line, this will be a snap.

1 Determine how wide you want the border to be. Cut your fabric into 4 strips of this width in the length of your duvet cover plus the width of the border. Remember to add 1 inch for seam allowance. For the bottom of the border, measure the width of the duvet. Cut 2 strips in this width plus the width of the border and remember to add 1 inch for seam allowance.

2 Place one width strip and one length strip on top of each other with the right sides facing each other. Diagonally fold the corner to create a miter. With an iron, press the fold into place, then flatten the pieces back out.

3 Now stitch, keeping the right sides together, along the pressed fold line.

4 Trim the excess and press open the seam. Repeat on the other corners.

5 Place the top and bottom of the border with the right sides together. Stitch around the outside perimeter. Turn right side out and press open.

6 Matching the duvet cover and your border's right sides together, stitch the border to the edge of the duvet cover.

IT'S A STRETCH! ART ON A BUDGET

Wallpaper? I don't think so. Need to create interest or texture? Want to absorb sound? Add a custom focal point to a room? This demo offers a chic, custom, layered adornment using wooden frames made from inexpensive artists' canvas stretchers. They're available to you, too, and they come in lengths of up to 8 feet. In our Town room (page 42) this project made the space seem truly custom. And you can adapt it in a number of ways. Large frames can be the perfect devices to separate living spaces or make instant foyers.

This project, including shopping, should take just a few hours.

(page 42)

MATERIALS AND TOOLS

Curtain rod

Cup hooks

Chain links

S-hooks

Stretchers (from the art supply store)

Paint (if the fabric is sheer)

Fabric

Scissors

Staple gun and staples

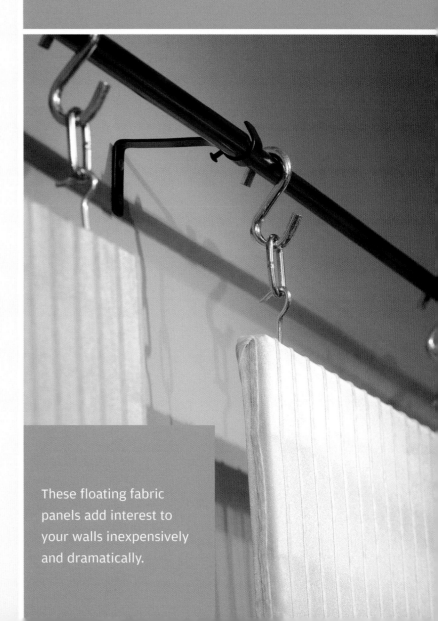

These floating fabric panels add interest to your walls inexpensively and dramatically.

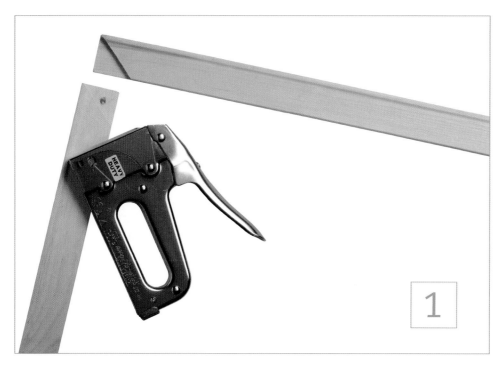

1

Start with a center staple on each of the four sides, then flip the frame over to make sure the fabric is positioned correctly. Then turn it facedown again and continue stapling. Trim any excess fabric that might show from the front. Hang the panels the way you'd hang an ordinary picture, or to duplicate our method, install an inexpensive curtain rod along the wall or walls you are treating. Screw two small cup hooks to the top of each frame and use simple chain links and S-hooks to attach the frames to the rod.

1 Assemble the frames by fitting the stretchers together at right angles. Some instructions recommend reinforcing the corners with nails or staples.

2 Paint the frames if you are covering them with sheer fabric. We painted ours the same color as the walls, but feel free to choose a contrasting color. If you're using an opaque fabric, there's no need to paint the frame.

3 Lay out your fabric facedown and place the frame facedown on top. Cut the fabric around the frame, leaving about a 3-inch border. You can always go back and trim the excess.

4 Using a staple gun, stretch the fabric over the side of the frame and staple it onto the back:

4

2

4

THE ART OF MERCHANDISING

The trick to great merchandising is to know when to stop. Remember, great taste is generally characterized by the art of restraint. Here all the accessories were chosen from mass-market stores in neighborhoods like yours. But every object was either organic—to add that natural touch—or it had a simple, clean, contemporary attitude to keep the space feeling modern. What's more important is to love everything you display and let it serve your vision and tell your story accurately.

ROOM SERVICE, PLEASE

Like any good hotel suite, a place for wine, glasses, plates, coffee, and snacks makes one feel pampered and provided for. Items like a small fridge and coffeemaker in or near the bedroom allow you that first glass of juice and a cup of joe without having to don your bathrobe and go trotting to the other side of the house to the kitchen.

OTTOMATIC, AUTOMATIC

In mass-market stores all over the place, retailers are finally offering ready-to-assemble cubes that can be used in a variety of ways. These flexible babies can be stacked to create an entire storage unit (see page 34) or stood up on their own as extra seating in a pinch. We chose the latter. If you learn to use batting, foam, and fabric to upholster, you'll be able to achieve a finished, custom look you can be proud of—and one that will work wonders for your budget.

This project, including shopping, should take just a few hours.

MATERIALS AND TOOLS

1 ready-to-assemble storage cube

Pencil

1 sheet of luan (¼-inch plywood)

Jigsaw

Upholstery foam

Batting

Scissors

Adhesive spray

Fabric

Staple gun and staples

Drill

Screws

1 Put together your cube by following the manufacturer's instructions. Our goal is to turn it into an ottoman by upholstering it for additional tush-cush.

2 Trace the top of the cube onto a piece of luan. Cut out the luan using a jigsaw or have the hardware store do it.

3 At your fabric shop or hobby store, purchase enough 1-inch cushion foam to fit each top. Pick up a roll of batting, too.

4 Cut the cushion foam to the size of the luan.

5 Give the luan and one side of the cushion a thin mist of low-tack adhesive spray and let it set for a minute or so. Then press the cushion foam onto the top of the luan. This will keep it in place for the next two steps.

6 Lay your foam-covered luan facedown on a section of batting. Cut the batting ¼ inch bigger than the top, all the way around. Another mist of adhesive will keep the batting in place while you cut. The batting will not wrap the top but will simply soften the luan edges once the fabric goes on.

7 Spread your upholstery fabric facedown and cut it at least 1½ inches larger on each side than the luan, foam, and batting top. You need enough to grip firmly and pull over the foam and batting, then staple to the back. You can always trim off the excess.

8 Position the fabric and cushion facedown and fold each side of the fabric over to the backside of the luan. Begin at the center of each side and attach with one staple per side, then turn it over to make sure the fabric is positioned the way you want it. Adjust if necessary.

9 Continue stapling your way around. I like a staple every 2 inches or so. When you get to the corners, ease the fabric a little at a time or simply fold the fabric neatly to make a single, diagonal pleat at each corner. Trim away excess fabric.

10 Now place the cushion on top of the cube and secure the top in place from the underside with screws long enough to grab the plywood but not long enough to poke through to the batting and foam. Hey, you're done!

Portable and versatile, these simple padded boxes become a bench at the foot of a bed or an extra pull-up seat for company.

A plain-Jane pair of ready-to-assemble chests of drawers gets a glam makeover with a two-tone paint job and towel-bar handles from the local bed and bath store. That's a lot of bling, baby.

VARIATION

Towel bars used both vertically and horizontally dress up crackle-finished kitchen cabinets.

MIRROR MAGIC

Lining the backs of the shelves with mirrors gives the illusion that this solid bed surround is see-through.

BUILDING UP, NOT OUT

It's one of my favorite decorating solutions: If you can't build out, build up. Here, two 6-foot ready-made floating shelves create a ledge at eye level much like a fireplace mantel. Even though everything on this wall comes from different places, the color of the black shelves repeated in the storage units below creates a harmonious, almost built-in look that is clean and sleek.

ADAPTATION: GENDER BENDER

A great resource for ideas can be found at your local sewing shop in the pattern department. Our friends at Jo-Ann Stores used this pattern with these fabrics to create a whole new look.

8898

ONE SIZE
UNA TALLA SOLA
UNE SEULE TAILLE

0 39363 23284 1

Simplicity
HOME
BEDDING BASICS

While the bed structure remains the same, simply changing out the bed ensemble gives our bedroom area a whole new feminine sensibility. Never underestimate the power of fabric.

OPEN TO THE PUBLIC: SHARED SPACES

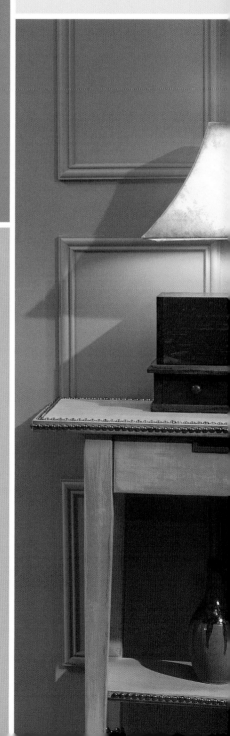

Decorating public, high-traffic spaces like dens, family rooms, and kitchens can be tricky. If they are all visible to one another, they may have to be "read" as one large space. With today's trend toward less formal rooms and more flexible, open spaces, it becomes even more important to unify, define, and design living areas that work both from a practical point of view and a visual one.

This tract-house kitchen and family room/center hall combo provided just such a challenge. These multi-functioning spaces must work hard as the primary communal living space—often for the entire household. And with one big, open environment, even knowing where to stop and start paint color can be hard. Then the kitchen itself—the money pit of the house—can present a variety of other hassles. For instance, how does one

No architecture in sight? Watch how this wall becomes the room's focal point.

deal with built-in countertops and inherited cabinets that might be too costly to replace but are in definite need of an upgrade? This is where being clever and developing a few do-it-yourself skills can save the day and a lot of money. Anytime there are elements in rooms that don't mesh, the art of disguise can work very well.

This particular room had some good elements: a nice sofa and upholstered chairs and a very respectable armoire. The color of the sofa, however, seemed wrong for the rest of the space, as the pale chartreuse appeared nowhere else in the room. But we loved the color and decided to look for ways to tie it in elsewhere, not only for visual balance (as the eye always goes to color) but to make the sofa look as though it really had been purchased for the room instead of having been left over from "the last house," which indeed it was.

The dining room table and chairs, although sturdy, left much to be desired aesthetically. Rather than looking "country," they simply looked old-fashioned and dated. The breakfast/dining area was, to say the least, underwhelming, and the windows were off, underscale, and shoved into the room's corner. The windows were diminished further by valances encroaching on what little there was left of the exposed glass and light. So we'd have to redo the window treatments to create the illusion that the windows were much bigger and therefore more in scale with the kitchen and den area.

In fact, that entire corner seemed underutilized, ill defined, and lackluster. We immediately thought of creating a structure that would not only feel built in but also provide storage, architectural interest, and purpose to what ultimately would be a visually important area in the room. The idea of a country-style hutch combined with a restaurant-style banquette provided the perfect solution. What's more, these details would also enhance the theme. But without a big budget or advanced carpentry skills, we would have to rely on ready-made and store-bought items that could be inexpensively embellished. Then with a little imagination we would spot items intended for one use and apply them to another. Keeping your objectives clear will help you discover or sometimes even invent the solution to your decorating dilemma.

Once we had a game plan to address the big things in the room, we actually could focus on the little things that weren't working as well as they could. It is always good to look for any way to simplify and streamline.

While the message center between the window and the kitchen cabinets is practical, it is also cluttered looking, so we would rather not see it from the sitting area. Speaking of kitchen cabinets, these do little for the space. But by adding molding, we might be able to beef them up a bit. And by minimizing the contrast

BEFORE

1   COLOR PALETTE

Saturated colors of persimmon, mustard, and sage will work for period rooms as well as for today's more casual contemporary looks.

We always start with our paint colors, here Creamed Asparagus and Clay Cotta for the walls, and Peas and Cream for the trim. We'll use the colors to minimize the contrast between the existing stained cabinets and the stark white walls. We'll beef up the look of the cabinets by adding crown moldings in the same finish.

2   ATTITUDE

Bead board screams "country hutch." We'll add this to our walls as an architectural embellishment and we'll paint it sage. It's also a subtle way to add geometry to a space.

3   ACCENTS

Our accent fabric contains all the colors we will be using in the room. Dusty green Ultrasuede will handle the upholstery and pillows, while a textured green woven will work for the window treatments and won't compete with our accent stripe.

Accessories will include a set of pale green dishes to adorn a plate rack, which will line the bead-board walls.

4   TEXTURE

Inexpensive rope and twine will embellish more accessories while adding yet another texture to the room.

Trimming with a nail-head kit dresses up both the hallway and dining room tables. Since it comes on a roll, it is easy to apply and takes a fraction of the time it would take to apply individual brass tacks.

PAD

PLATE RACK
OVER BUILT iN
SEATING

MARBLEIZE
COUNTER
TOP

PicTURE
FRAMES

between the wall and cabinet colors, we could also help integrate the cabinets into their surroundings.

The countertops in the kitchen were made of a strange blue-gray laminate. They either had to be coordinated with the room or chucked out completely. To keep the cost down, I would use my marbleizing technique right over the existing countertop, allowing us to incorporate the room's colors.

And about the wall color—where is it? Rich wall color will add drama and definition to these spaces. The wall hiding the other half of the kitchen, the one with the console table in front, is important and should become a focal point. Here again, adding architectural elements would give the wall substance and presence. But to mind our budget, we'd have to use ready-made elements.

A simple picture frame used in multiples might be a solution, giving the wall a raised-panel effect. Molding is molding, whether it frames a picture or a wall. Applying a grid of store-bought photo frames to the wall is a darn sight easier than measuring, mitering, and gluing sixty angles together and hoping they'll all come out right, right? If you have a small budget and poor substitutes threaten to compromise your vision, a few designer skills and a clever eye will help you reach your final goal.

This plain tract-house kitchen and family room has a whole new attitude and charm with an easy-to-do banquette, a few window and shelf treatments, and a paint job with plenty of visual punch.

picture frames

GO BOLD!

The new rich color minimizes the contrast between the walls and the kitchen cabinets while unifying the entire space.

Our built-in banquette began with two ready-to-assemble "Lack" units from Ikea, placed on their sides along perpendicular walls. On top of each we added a piece of MDF (medium-density fiberboard) to create the base where the cushion will later go.

From that point up to the ceiling, we nailed sheets of bead board to the wall, notching out around the window cases. The pros would have removed the window casings altogether, but that is so much trouble! Instead, we applied half-round molding between the bead board and the window casing . . . much easier and less disruptive to the walls. At the ceiling and bead-board edges we applied decorative, prepainted foam molding for a nice custom-look finish.

Premade gallery ledge molding (purchased in lumber supply stores, The Home Depot, Lowe's, etc.) was then cut to create the display shelves, which are secured with screws to the bead board.

The bead board, decorative foam molding, and embellishments to the tops of the existing kitchen cabinets all combine to give this space an architectural makeover.

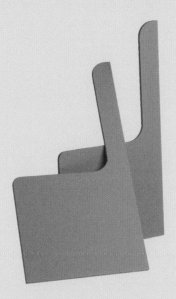

Home Base

Out of MDF we created the banquette ends using a cardboard template and a jigsaw. To make the template, we positioned the cardboard at one end of the banquette and traced the shape to clear the seat cushion and the back bolster by about an inch. We cut out the template, then placed the template on the MDF and cut the two end pieces with a jigsaw. The pieces were then sanded, painted, and screwed in.

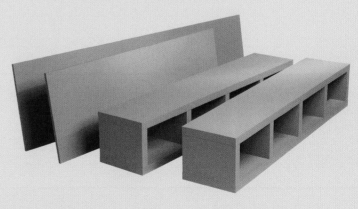

BOLSTER YOUR ROOM'S EGO

FOR THE BACK BOLSTERS, YOU WILL NEED

6 sheets of luan (1/4-inch plywood), cut to fit the flat sides of the foam

Spray adhesive

6 equal lengths of half-round foam

Fabric

Staple gun and staples

Industrial-strength Velcro (available at larger hardware centers)

1 Spray the luan pieces on one side with adhesive and apply to the flat sides of the foam half-rounds.

2 To upholster, wrap the fabric around all sides of the foam and secure it in the back using a staple gun.

3 To install, staple one part of industrial-strength Velcro to the wall and the corresponding part to the wood back of the finished cushion.

Here we've used the same bolster idea, but as a window topper.

LET'S GET CUSHY

SEWING LESSON

1 Determine the seat size and have foam cut to the measurements. Cut two fabric pieces the width and length of the foam plus 1 inch for seam allowance. These are the top and bottom of the cushion cover.

2 Cut pieces for the sides. Don't forget to include a 1-inch seam allowance.

3 Pin the sides to the top and bottom. Stitch the cover, right sides together, on three sides, leaving an opening in the back big enough to insert the foam.

4 Trim the corners and turn the cover right side out.

5 Insert the foam and hand sew the opening.

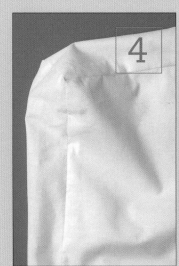

DON'T GET CARRIED AWAY

When dealing with high-ticket upholstery or built-ins, it is best to choose solid colors and classic textures rather than prints or trendy fabrics, which can be the first things to date a room. Let your pillows be the decorative accents, as they are easily (and affordably) changed, while your sofa remains timeless.

PIPING

Piping adds that "designer" touch. Here we added it to the pillows, but it can also be added to seat cushions, slipcovers, pillowcases, duvets . . .

This is how it's done:

1 Find the bias by folding fabric on a 45-degree diagonal.

2 Cut the fabric into strips wide enough to allow for the diameter of the piping cord plus seam allowance.

3 Place the cord in the center of the fabric strip and fold in half, right sides out. Using a zipper foot attachment on your sewing machine, sew along the cord.

You did it!

SEWING LESSON

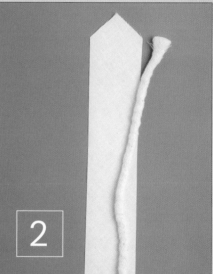

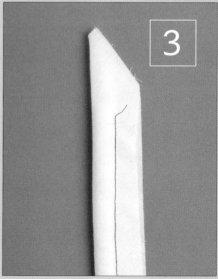

PAINT YOUR WAY OUT OF THE PAST

We often feel that we can't afford to move forward with our decorating due to inherited eyesores, such as ugly kitchen countertops. Here, using the wall, trim, and accent colors already in the room, we faux marbled the counter-top to blend beautifully with the new décor.

MARBLEIZING

If you've ever looked at some of the marbleizing kits available on the market, you know that you can barely pronounce the names of the ingredients, much less know what to do with all of them. And they cost a fortune!

Well, I've developed an easy, easy, easy marbleizing technique that you can do using ordinary latex house paint, masking tape, and a paintbrush. Follow these easy steps and you'll be marbleizing in no time.

This project can take anywhere from an hour to a few days. It all depends on the item being covered. Our counter was done over two days, because the paint needs to dry thoroughly before the polyurethane can be applied.

MATERIALS AND TOOLS

Stain-blocking primer
(such as Bin or Kilz)

Latex house paint in
3 shades of one color
family

3 small containers, for
holding the paint

Wood panel to practice on

Pencil

Masking tape or painter's
tape

4-inch-wide paintbrush

1 small artist's brush, for
painting "veins" (optional)

Water-based, nonyellowing
polyurethane

1 roller, paintbrush, or
foam brush, for
polyurethane

Fine-grit sandpaper

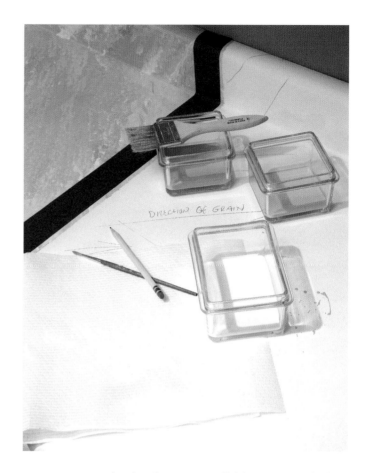

Here are the basics as we did it on an existing laminated countertop:

The paint store has made it supersimple for you to choose the colors for this technique. You'll see a display of paint swatches, and all you need to do is choose a color you like. On any paint swatch, take the darkest color, the lightest color, and the medium color, and that's all you need to get started. Purchase semigloss, eggshell, or satin paint. Don't use flat or high-gloss paint.

1 Prime the entire surface of the countertop using a product designed for nonporous surfaces. Coat the underside lip of the counter as well. Let dry.

2 Pour small amounts of each paint color into individual containers.

3 The seams are the most important part of the illusion of marble. (You might want to practice first on a wooden panel.) To divide the counter into even sections, draw a pencil line down the center horizontally and vertically. In each section, draw diagonal lines to indicate the direction of the grain pattern. Alternate the direction of the lines in each adjacent section. At the seams, the direction of the painting will change to look like blocks of marble are positioned next to each other.

4 Mask off one of the sections using masking tape or painter's tape along both sides of the quadrant. Be sure the tape is stuck onto the wood really well so no paint will seep through the edge. Work in only one section at a time.

5 Dip a 4-inch paintbrush into each color to begin. Load up a little bit of each color. Painting *only* in the direction of the lines you've drawn, use a combination of front-to-back and stippling motions. Continue to "grab" colors to add contrast within the section. Add a little more of the lighter color to contrast with the dark. Blend the edges of the colors with the brush. You don't want a line of demarcation between the colors.

6 As soon as you've finished the square, immediately remove the masking or painter's tape.

7 When the paint dries, tape off the next square by positioning the tape just slightly beyond the paint line of the adjacent square so there will be a little overlap of the paint in both squares.

8 Load the three colors on the brush and work in the opposite direction of the first block so the illusion is that the grain is creating a seam between two marble blocks. Keep picking up colors of paint onto the brush and remember to work only in one direction, "pouncing" and stippling.

9 When you are finished, immediately remove the tape. Let this square dry and move on to the next.

10 If you like, you can add veining to the "marble." Dip a small artist's brush into the darkest and lightest colors. Use a random pulling-then-turning motion to create the vein. Dip the brush again and add an offshoot of the vein from the first stroke. Blend the vein slightly by pouncing over it with the 4-inch brush. Remove the tape while the paint is still wet.

11 Apply the polyurethane. This adds that layer of luster that makes the marbleizing look very convincing. I have found this works best when the painted surface is allowed to dry overnight first, and when you apply at least two coats of polyurethane. The first coat is usually rough. Lightly sand the surface—just enough to roughen it a bit so the polyurethane will adhere. Apply the polyurethane in one direction only, from top to bottom, using either a roller, a paintbrush, or a foam brush. If you're applying polyurethane to a wall, choose a stopping point to make a seam halfway down the wall. Then apply the polyurethane the rest of the way, always working from top to bottom. Let dry. Lightly sand and add additional coats. I've found that three to four coats usually works best.

There you have it. Quick and simple. Now think of all the things you can marbleize—from wooden candle holders to countertops to columns to walls and floors. Use your imagination and add a rich look for a fraction of the cost.

PAINT ABUSE: DISTRESSING

Using the two colors chosen for our new room, we painted this flea-market table and the ready-to-assemble hall table. We painted them first in persimmon and let them dry completely. Then we painted over them with the apple green. When that dried, we simply sanded through the top coat in patches to reveal the "old" layer of persimmon paint beneath.

MATERIALS AND TOOLS

Primer paint (optional)

2 paint colors

Heavy-grit sandpaper

Tack-cloth

Paintbrushes

Water-based, nonyellowing polyurethane

To coordinate the old chairs with the newly distressed dining table, we painted them a solid color. We also reupholstered each chair by removing the seats, adding foam padding, and stapling the fabric underneath the seat. We used the same fabric as for the window treatment, which helped bring the pattern from the window into the center of the alcove.

1 Prime the object (use Bin or Kilz if you are working with a nonporous material such as glass, plastic, or laminate).

2 Choose two colors, one as a base color and one as the top color. The top color, obviously, will be the one you see most, with the base color peeking through in the "distressed" spots.

3 Sand the object well and wipe it clean with a tack-cloth. Prime if desired.

4 Paint the object with your base color and allow it to dry thoroughly overnight.

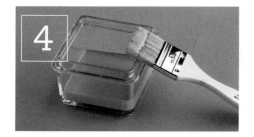

5 Paint the top color over the base color, and again, allow it to dry overnight. If the paint is not completely dry, it will be too soft to sand.

6 In a random fashion with the sandpaper, rub through the top coat to reveal the accent paint color beneath. Step back now and then to evaluate. This technique is virtually mistake-proof; the more you sand, the better it looks. For a more authentic effect, sand edges and areas that would become worn with repeated use.

7 If you want to protect your finish, apply two or three coats of polyurethane, letting each coat dry thoroughly before applying the next.

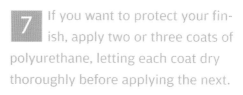

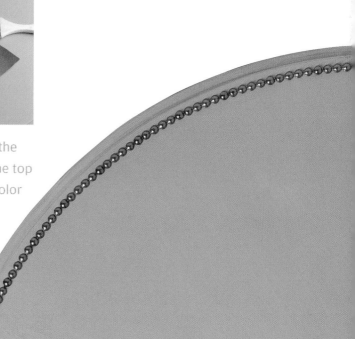

VARIATION

You can create endless combinations. Here's a terra-cotta base coat and a blue top coat.

This example uses the distressing technique with a crackle finish. For another idea using a crackle finish, see page 145.

A crackle finish saves this
downtrodden floor, putting it
back into "check."

ARCHITECTURE FOUND!

To dress up an important wall, we bought twenty inexpensive picture frames and used liquid nails to mount them to the wall in a grid pattern. Then we painted everything the same color. It's a great and easy way to get the raised panel look of fine carpentry for a fraction of the cost.

Picture frames, glue, and paint. Who knew?

BEFORE

AFTER

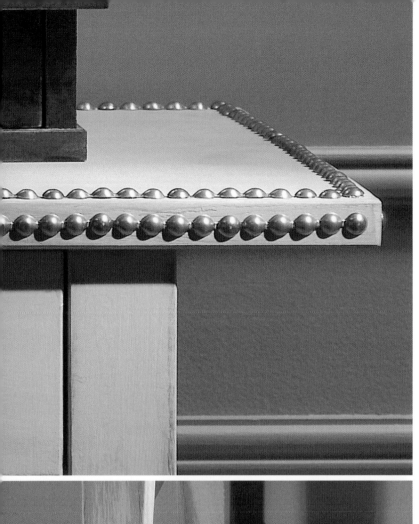

Embracing the art of disguise will also help to move along your projects. When you use ordinary, ready-to-assemble furniture and embellish it for your own custom look, decorating becomes fun. Meaning, you don't have to know how to build a table, a countertop, a chair, a bookcase . . . you just need to know how to make it better by customizing it with simple elements like paint, fabric, trims, and the myriad notions available at your local craft store. When you apply your creativity, you make whatever you touch one of a kind—like you!

As a finishing touch, we studded the table edge and legs with nail heads using a cool nail-head trim kit we found at our local Jo-Ann store. It comes on a roll for easy application. . . .
Love that.

LET THERE BE LAMP

This country-chic lamp began as a single unfinished box and drawer from the hobby store. We glued the plywood box on top of the drawer.

After the glue dried, we stained them both with a mahogany glaze. Using a lamp kit, we drilled a cord hole in the back of the box and another in the top center of the box. We assembled the rest of the lamp kit according to the directions, which are a snap, and gave it a store-bought simple parchment shade.

VASES ON THE ROPES

By using one simple element in an unconventional way, you can often transform a boring object into a beautiful one. In this case ordinary rope turned a clear glass cylinder into that final custom accessory for one of our room redos. We used the same elements with two different applications. Use braid, trims, and fringes to embellish everything from lamp bases to covered boxes. But remember, less is best for a more sophisticated look.

These projects, including shopping, should take only a few hours.

VASE #1

MATERIALS AND TOOLS

Hot-glue gun

Yellow high-temperature hot-glue sticks

Spool of thin rope

2 glass cylinder vases (one to fit inside the other with space for the rope)

Scissors

VASE #2

Hot-glue gun

Yellow high-temperature hot-glue sticks

Rope (use any type or thickness of rope you like)

Glass cylinder vase

Scissors

1 Using the hot glue, attach one end of the rope to the bottom of the larger glass cylinder and carefully coil the rope around the inside of the cylinder until you reach the top. Once the rope is flush to the top of the cylinder, cut it and tack that end of the rope in place with a dot of glue.

2 Insert the smaller cylinder into the larger one. This internal cylinder is what you'll use to hold water and flowers.

1 Using the hot glue, attach one end of the rope to the outside of the cylinder base and wind your way up, liberally dabbing the vase with glue to keep the rope in place. Once you reach the top of the cylinder, cut the rope and tack it in place with a dot of glue.

2 Another idea is to create a "cuff" effect by winding the rope only around the top and bottom of the vase using the same glue-as-you-go method described above.

ADAPTATION:
OUT ON A WHIM

At any large mass-market store, you might find light fixtures like the ones we used here, three identical and fairly nondescript hanging lights. We covered the shades and cords with leftover pillow fabric, and wow!

See how just changing the window and pillow fabrics gives the room a completely different attitude?

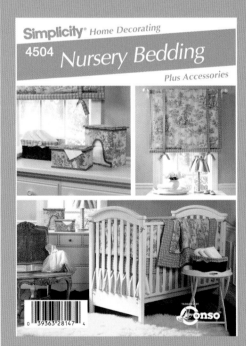

Simplicity® Home Decorating

4504 *Nursery Bedding*

Plus Accessories

0 39363 28147 4

SEXY SPACES: MASTERING THE MASTER

I could write volumes on the master bedroom alone. Certainly we have done many a TV show on the topic. Think of it: a room that has to be both comfortable and restful, practical and pretty, public and private, *and* accommodate two people's individual tastes. Suffice it to say, it is the most intimate and personal space to decorate in the entire home. And as a result, sometimes bedrooms do not get done at all. Or at best they are postponed until the public spaces are finished. As I have said and written many times, your bedroom is where you begin and end each day; therefore, how you feel in it is important. Your master bedroom should be done ASAP and with as much time and attention as you pay to your living room. Pamper yourself. You deserve it. That's why you work so hard!

It used to be that fine bed linens were unaffordable to many, and three-hundred-thread-count sheets were for the rich. Not so anymore. Thanks to global resources, today, fine linens, down pillows, blanket covers, and comforters are not only affordable, they are essential. I say "essential" because they

can literally transform the bed into a veritable oasis. And what about an oasis is not to love, want, and need? Do you hear me?

The bed is often the biggest thing in the room and should be played up luxuriously. In fact, in many four- and five-star hotels, when you enter the room, the bed is already turned down in order to show off the crisply ironed sheets and downy soft pillows. Gone are the froufrou throw pillows and the floral, quilted bedspreads in favor of a look that emphasizes texture and tailoring much like a finely crafted suit, or should I say suite?

When we tackled this bedroom, we wanted it, when finished, to reflect a modern sensibility that today's young couples would appreciate and enjoy. We wanted the space to be tailored enough for him, which meant keeping things straightforward with easy, uncomplicated lines. For her we wanted to create the feel of luxury. Our research tells us that she will tend to compromise in terms of pattern and design as long as the "snuggle factor" is maintained. In other words, favoring texture over pattern might keep peace between the sexes. Oddly enough, when we asked many couples where they were getting their design ideas, they said from their favorite hotels and restaurants. And it makes sense. Commercial designers nowadays are careful to keep spaces gender neutral, especially when there are nearly as many women traveling as there are men. Hoteliers want their lobbies and rooms to be hip and yet still businesslike, exemplified by places like the W and Four Seasons hotels across the country. So "check in" with us to see how some of these upscale-hotel design ideas have been used to bring heart, soul, and hipness into a dull and lifeless bedroom.

The room's cold white walls need to be warmed up right off the bat and decorated more effectively to give the room a point of view. You'll be surprised at how strong, rich wall color can add to the atmosphere and intimacy of a bedroom, offering drama and sensuality. But often our fear of color holds us back and then

1 ATTITUDE

Clean, sleek, and chic, this dull room gets a five-star-hotel-suite makeover.

2 COLOR PALETTE

It's all about contrast. While this palette is not truly monochromatic, it spans a limited color range and is therefore easy to work with.

Starting with the shell of the room, a coat of Dried Blueberry from the Christopher Lowell paint collection transforms the dimensions of a small white space. For the trim and architectural embellishments, Navy Bean will begin the stark contrast story. Painting patterns in diamond shapes will add a built-in geometry to the drapery cornices and to the eventual headboard.

3 TEXTURE

To keep the room sexy and sleek, layers of suede in medium green, dark putty, and cream continue the contrast story in fabric.

Clean white sheers will become the focal point for the window treatments, contrasting against the deep-colored walls. Crisp white bed linens will carry that color into the center of the room.

The bed pillows will contrast with the mattress cover in a khaki herringbone with dark suede insets. This combination appears again to cover the bookcases, pulling that element back to the shell of the room.

White faux fur will cover two retro bedside lamps, bringing in a fun, "fashion" element—albeit in small doses, as it should be.

Cinder blocks supporting the bed platform will also get painted a deep putty green to make them recede into the shell of the room while still providing a hint of texture.

4 ORGANIC ELEMENTS

Varying lengths of bamboo are clustered together to act as floral containers. Finished with silver leaf, they blend with the silver accents in the room.

5 ACCENTS

Chrome tea-light holders, glass shelf brackets, and a chrome reading lamp will act as the "jewelry" of the room, adding a modern sparkle to the otherwise subdued and tranquil background.

Can this room become:
- dual function?
- tranquil?
- non-gender specific?
- sexy?

we overspend on furniture in our attempts to bring warmth into the space. Don't be afraid of color! Especially in those rooms where the door is closed as much as it is open.

One of the ways to create a calming feeling in a bedroom is to keep it fairly monochromatic. This means keeping the range of colors to a minimum and focusing on lighter and darker shades of the same color. A simple tool to help you do this is a single strip of sample paint colors containing several shades of

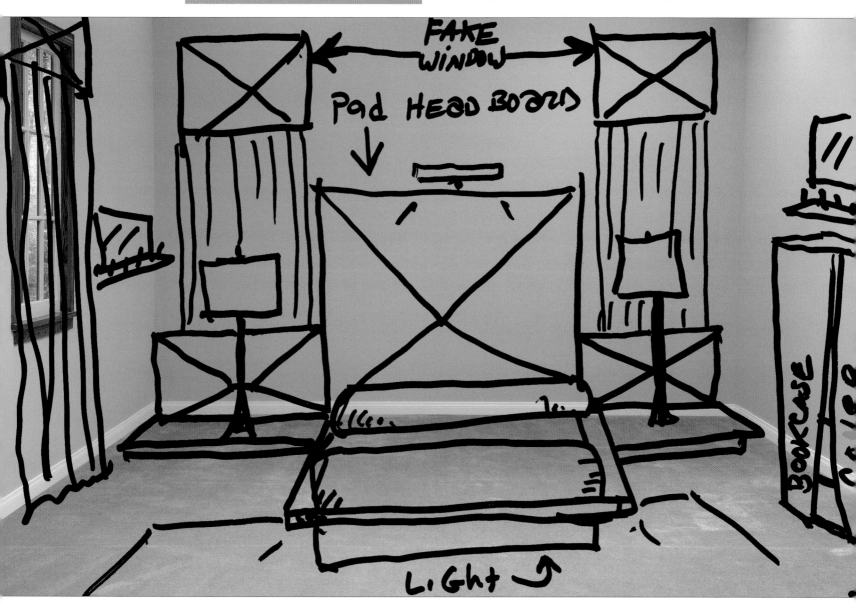

the same color, usually arranged from light to dark. Take this with you as you select everything from linens and lamp shades to storage containers, upholstery, and rugs. Also remember that fabric and carpet absorb sound, and a quiet bedroom is a peaceful, romantic haven. . . . Or it will be once we install that all-important mood lighting. Get rid of the cold overhead lights in favor of lamps and pin spotlights, with everything on dimmers. Shadow creates interest and atmosphere.

For bedrooms we favor subdued spa- and nature-inspired colors such as gray flannel, gray-blue, dark slate, taupe, chocolate, tan, and putty. These soothing shades are neither masculine nor feminine and are most likely to be conducive to sleep. Add the romance of candles and well . . . other activities suddenly seem appropriate.

The bedside dressers currently in this room are underscaled and impractical, and the lamps don't help, either. Perhaps combining the nightstands with the bed frame would achieve a built-in effect and would offer usable surface on each bedside. A matching pair of lamps would add more drama, symmetry, and function to the bed area.

The love seat seems to be taking up valuable wall space, while storage in the room is inadequate for two people. We'll need to address all these factors to decorate and customize this important space.

Making this master bedroom a place of serenity doesn't mean it has to be boring. There's still plenty of room to be playful. The great thing about a monochromatic color scheme is that all the elements will coordinate and be visually harmonious. For our wall color, let's go deep. Yes, I feel your skepticism, but I want to show you how well strong, rich wall color can work in a small space without closing it in. In my *Seven Layers of Design,* wall color is layer number one, the first design decision you make. The six layers following cover everything from carpeting to candlesticks, so the wall color may end up being a small part of the picture.

In the case of our bedroom here, only about a third of the walls will actually be visible when the room is complete. The dark flannel walls will work well in our color scheme, contrasting beautifully with cream tones and nicely playing up our crisp white accents. We wanted to reinterpret a sexy Hollywood–L.A. *Confidential* look with a modern twist. Get it?

JOIN THE CLUB

One master bedroom "must" is a comfortable upholstered piece to snuggle into. Our pair of matching club chairs is the most expensive thing in the room, but because we so economically dealt with the decorating, we felt we could splurge on the chairs. We chose a metallic geometric fabric with a hint of retro attitude to juxtapose with the chair's classic frame.

A:
Yes!

CUE LIGHTING . . .

For a sexy effect come nighttime, we installed rope lighting, which can be purchased in a kit at larger hardware stores. Using the clips that come with it, we attached the rope light to the underside of both the platform and the two side tables to underlight the entire structure.

Color Me Subtle

Take a look at our completed room. A once-drab stepchild of a space is now inviting and tranquil. Notice how each color is balanced evenly throughout. This allows the eye to travel naturally around the room. Even though the wall color is that deep gray, there is plenty of high-key cream and white to offset it. That's why knowing your seven layers and anticipating them will help you get over your fear of strong color. When you're looking to create an environment with high contrast, balance your colors by weaving them through the room to achieve visual harmony.

Once the walls were dry, we made three window cornices from ½-inch plywood. They were painted in a harlequin pattern using the gray wall color and the cream trim color already in the room. Why three cornices when there's only one window? We wanted to create the illusion of two more windows and make the one window seem twice as big as it was. We also wanted to create symmetry surrounding the bed.

So we hung two cornices on either side of the bed as close to the ceiling as possible. We did the same over the existing window. White sheers were installed inside the cornices, creating three columns of fabric. Now the illusion of three windows is complete.

A WINDOW'S ROYAL CROWN

This cornice technique is ideal for creating a window where there isn't one, or making a small window appear much bigger. It's a clever designer trick that should be a mainstay in your decorative home arts arsenal.

This project, including shopping, should take a full day.

MATERIALS AND TOOLS

Tape measure

½ sheet of medium-density fiberboard (MDF), ½ inch or ¾ inch thick

Jigsaw (or table saw if you have one)

Wood glue

Drill

Screws

Fabric (optional)

Batting (optional)

Trim or molding (optional)

Primer

Straightedge

Pencil

Painter's tape

2 paint colors

2 paintbrushes

Curtains

2 door-panel rods, with screws and drywall anchors

2 L-brackets

1 Measure your window's width. Decide how much more you want to visually increase the illusion of your existing window's width and height. In this example, for the height, we've added 3 more inches to both sides and measured from the ceiling to 3 inches below the top window molding (but with other windows in the past we've sometimes added up to a foot on both depending on the scale of the room). The part you just calculated is the front piece. To determine the depth of the cornice, measure how far out your rod and brackets come from the wall and add ½ inch to the depth for clearance. This allows space between the cornice and the drape. You now have your side dimensions. The top measurement is determined from the width and depth.

2 sing these measurents, cut one front, one top, and two sides of the cornice box out of MDF. (Most lumber departments will do this for you at about a dollar per cut.)

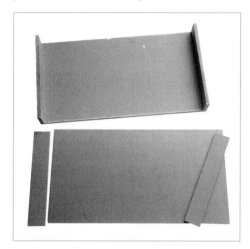

3 First glue the joints and then reinforce them with screws. You can now upholster the cornice with fabric and batting or embellish it with trim or molding. We simply painted it using two colors in a diamond pattern.

4 If you want to paint, first prime the cornice. Then, with a straightedge and a pencil, draw a line from the upper corner of one side of the cornice to the lower corner of the other, and repeat with the other two corners. You should have

two lines that intersect in the center of your cornice. Using your pencil line as your guide, tape diagonally corner to corner with painter's tape. Paint your first color in the two opposite triangles. Remove the tape immediately and let the paint dry.

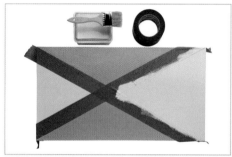

5 Tape off sections corner-to-corner, allowing for a small seam overlap where the two colors meet. Paint the remaining triangles with your second color. Remove the tape and let the paint dry. Repeat this step for the two sides of the cornice. Then paint the cornice top with whichever color you choose.

6 For the curtains, we hung store-bought sheer panels on door-panel rods, installing the rods on the wall with screws and drywall anchors.

7 To install the cornice, use two L-brackets mounted to the wall, so the top of the L sticks out from the wall at a right angle. Place the cornice on top of the brackets and secure with screws.

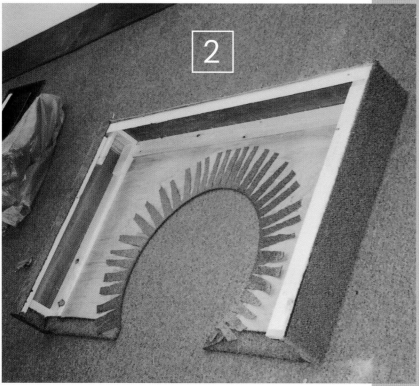

VARIATION

If you modify this technique by cutting a circle out and adding fabric, the result has a whole new attitude. Scale it down and add an arch. This project can take on more looks than Cher.

1 To create this look, measure the length of the cornice and subtract 12 inches (6 inches on both sides). Use this measurement as the diameter of a half-circle arch of luan approximately 3 inches wide. This is the frame of the arch.

2 Prime, paint, and attach as is, or cover with fabric as we did here. You'll need a piece of fabric about 2 inches longer than the arc of your arch and about 4 inches wider, to give you enough fabric to fold and staple over the sides. Notch the fabric toward the edes of the arc and staple.

3 To install the cornice, use two L-brackets mounted to the wall so that the top of the L sticks out from the wall at a right angle. Place the cornice on top of the brackets and secure with screws.

MARSHMALLOW MAGIC

We liked this faux poodle fur so much that we used it to cover the shades of the groovy-mod lamps flanking the bed. We painted the bases to match the room's trim. And they're high enough to be practical for reading in bed. You can do the same thing with leftover fabric, a plush cotton towel, or even a pillowcase.

HEAVENLY HEADBOARD

If you take away nothing else from this book, the absolute best way to give your home that designer feel is by applying a few simple techniques of upholstery. And nothing says "custom" like a sophisticated, padded headboard made especially for your bed. This simple and easy technique is used throughout the book in a variety of ways. Here, we show you how to create an oversized headboard. Instead of one large board, we divided it into four sections, which makes for much easier handling. This headboard is designed to affix directly to the wall, hotel-style.

This project, including shopping, should take a full day.

MATERIALS AND TOOLS

Tape measure

1 sheet of luan (¼-inch plywood)

Jigsaw

Batting

Scissors

Spray adhesive

Fabric

Staple gun and staples

Industrial-strength Velcro (available at larger hardware centers)

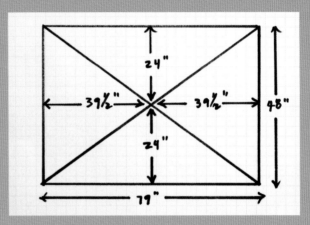

1 Measure your mattress and determine the dimensions of your headboard. It could be slightly wider or a lot wider than your mattress, depending on the effect you're going for. The trend for headboards today is taller and wider. If you want the headboard to encompass any side tables or platforms, allow for them as well. Refer to these measurements when purchasing the fabric.

Once you've determined the size and shape of your headboard, divide the completed shape into four sections diagonally.

2 Either have your lumberyard cut the four pieces out of ¼-inch luan or do it yourself with a jigsaw.

3 Cover each triangular piece separately with sheets of batting from your local fabric store. Lay the piece down on several layers of batting, depending on how much padding you want, and cut the batting, leaving a ¼-inch border all the way around. A little low-tack spray adhesive can hold the batting in place while you work.

Spread out your chosen fabric facedown, lay the padded wood facedown on top of that, and trim the fabric, leaving about a 3-inch border all around. Better to err on the side of caution; you can always trim further.

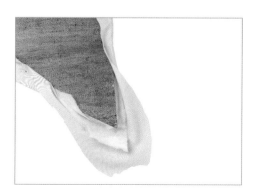

4 Begin stapling the fabric in place by doing a starter staple in the center of each side for positioning. When you are happy with the fabric's placement, finish stapling. Repeat the steps above with the other three pieces.

5 Once all four pieces are finished, you're ready to assemble them into one big shape. Hint: It's not a bad idea to trace the finished shapes onto the wall. This will act as a guide for installation.

Using peel-and-stick industrial-strength Velcro, cut a strip nearly the length of each side of each piece. So if your pieces are triangles, you will have three strips of Velcro for each triangle.

Peel off the sticky side of each Velcro strip and stick it along the edge of the wood back of each padded piece. Now staple the strips for reinforcement.

Using your pencil marks on the wall for guidance, stick the corresponding Velcro strips to the wall where the headboard will go. Staple to reinforce those as well.

When all four headboard sections and corresponding wall locations have their Velcro, attach the sections to the wall, fitting them snugly together.

You can leave as is or add molding on all three sides or even a picture ledge on top. You decide! In this example, we added battery-powered picture lights.

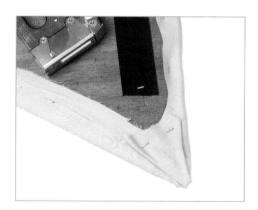

VARIATIONS

For a quick and easy headboard, attach Velcro to the back of store-bought pillows and affix them to the wall.

Cut a piece of luan into squares. Apply batting on top and cover with a fabric. Attach the squares to the wall with Velcro. Voilà! Another one-of-a-kind project. For a dramatic effect in a hall, apply these squares from floor to ceiling. How cool.

FLOATING BED

For the bed, we wanted to create a built-in effect where the nightstands and the bed platform appear to be one single unit.

We began building the bed platform by placing cinder blocks on the floor in a large rectangle with the solid part of them facing out. The blocks had been painted in a color two shades darker than the walls, with the color chosen from the same paint strip as the wall color to ensure that the values went together. In the center of the rectangle we added another row of blocks as support for the platform. Our bed was a standard double measuring 54 by 72 inches. To be sure the platform provided ample surface room around the mattress, we used three hollow-core doors that were 28 inches wide by 80 inches long, painted the same color as the walls. The doors were laid next to one another horizontally on top of the cinder blocks.

For the nightstands we extended the cinder blocks, adding a row on either side of the bed to connect the bed platform to the left and right walls. Another hollow-core door was cut in half lengthwise and placed atop these blocks to form a 16-inch ledge on either side of the bed—and voilà, bedside tables!

A PLATFORM FOR CREATIVITY: ZEN BED

Naturally, the centerpiece of most bedrooms is the bed. This demo will show you a flexible and inexpensive way to give an ordinary mattress the five-star treatment. While this cinder-block base might remind you of your dorm-room days, our upgrade treatment won't.

This project, including shopping, should take a weekend.

MATERIALS AND TOOLS

Tape measure

Cinder blocks

Paint (for cinder blocks and hollow-core doors—can be different colors)

Thick-nap paint roller (for the cinder blocks)

Regular-nap paint roller (for the hollow-core doors)

Four 28-inch hollow-core doors

Flat metal brackets

Drill

Jigsaw

1 To make the platform base, measure your mattress, then calculate how many cinder blocks you will need to border the perimeter of the mattress and make a row down the middle for extra support. You want the base to be a little larger than the mattress. A standard double, like the one used here, is 54 inches by 72 inches. Standard cinder blocks measure 15 inches long, by 7$\frac{1}{2}$ inches wide, by 7$\frac{1}{2}$ inches deep. Eighteen blocks would do the trick. You may vary your dimensions, of course, just "block" it out accordingly!

2 If you want to lay out the base to check size and position before placing the actual blocks, make 15-inch by 7$\frac{1}{2}$-inch paper templates and place them on the floor where you want the bed to be. Trust me, it's much easier to move these around than it is to move around the blocks.

3 Paint all surfaces of the blocks that will show once the platform is complete. When in doubt, paint it. We used the darkest color from the same paint strip as the room's wall, trim, and ceiling colors, in an eggshell finish. Dark colors show fewer imperfections.

4 Now place the cinder blocks directly on the floor or carpet, following your template.

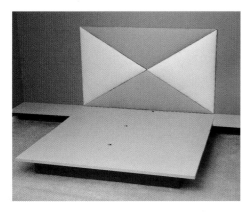

5 To create a platform that might also act as a ledge on which to set a drink, a magazine, or a remote control, you'll need to extend the platform surface beyond the sides of the mattress. For our purposes, three ready-made, lightweight hollow-core doors were perfect, as they measure 28 inches wide by 80 inches long.

6 Paint the doors. For ours, we used the same color as the walls of the room.

7 Lay the doors across the cinder blocks, centering them over the base, and attach the doors to one another with flat metal brackets. We used two flat brackets and attached them in the center of where each door meets.

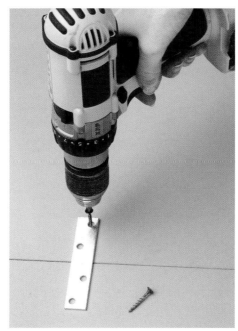

8 Beginning at the bed base, lay a single row of blocks end to end along the wall. Since our room was relatively small, we extended the blocks from wall to wall. The number of blocks will depend on the space from your bed base to the wall.

9 From another hollow-core door, use a jigsaw to cut two pieces measuring the width of the extension by 16 inches deep.

10 Attach these two side pieces to the bed platform using the same flat metal brackets you used for the platform.

COOL THREADS

A trend started by chic hotels is to show off the bed linens, which we've done here. But for a touch of whimsy and texture, we added a long body pillow covered in a fun white faux poodle fur. (This is the same fabric that we used to cover the lamp shades on page 109, remember?) And since the mattress is completely exposed, we used a box-style bed cover in gray faux suede with herringbone tweed insets. This, much like a fitted sheet, encases the mattress for a tailored look. Similar styles can be found at better home stores.

BAMB-BEAUTIFUL VASES

The primary ingredient here is 4-inch-diameter bamboo. Look for it in places like your neighborhood import stores, floral supply shops, or catalogs like Loose Ends (see the resource guide). Since it is a natural substance, dimensions will vary.

This project, including shopping, should take just a few hours.

MATERIALS AND TOOLS

4-inch-diameter bamboo stalks

Utility knife or small saw for cutting the bamboo and the bottles

Silver-leaf adhesive (available at your local craft store)

Soft-bristle craft brush

Peel-off silver-leaf sheets

Soft cloth

Small plastic water bottles

1 Begin by cutting the bamboo to desired lengths. Nestled in a cluster of three for visual effect, one good possibility is lengths of 5, 9, and 12 inches. But use your own judgment based on your specific needs.

2 With a craft brush, apply silver-leaf adhesive to each bamboo cylinder. Let it dry at least one hour, or until sticky to the touch. Too wet, and the silver leaf is difficult to work with; too dry, and it will not adhere.

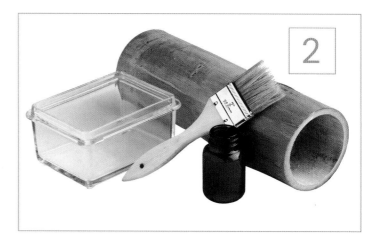

3 From a roll of peel-off silver-leaf sheets, cut sections the length of each piece of bamboo. Laying the bamboo piece on its side (working one side at a time), rub on the silver leaf with a dry soft cloth. Not all the silver leaf will stick, but that's okay. The goal is to leave silver highlights showing the natural bamboo underneath.

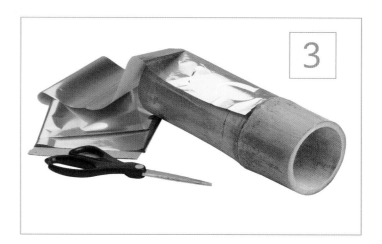

4 If you're going to fill the finished vase with fresh flowers, insert individual plastic water bottles into the bamboo openings (natural depths will vary). Mark where to cut the water bottle so the plastic container is flush with the top of the bamboo cylinder.

Silver or gold leafing is a great technique to have under your designer hat. It can add sparkle and drama to almost anything, from artificial fruit to ceilings.

Zen-sational Candle Ledges

Four inexpensive wardrobe mirrors, with their frames painted the color of the walls, rest horizontally on bracketed glass-shelf units mounted on the wall, adding a romantic glow to the room while creating the illusion of space. The tops of the mirrors are the same height as the top of the bed's headboard. The votive candles make a beautiful reflection.

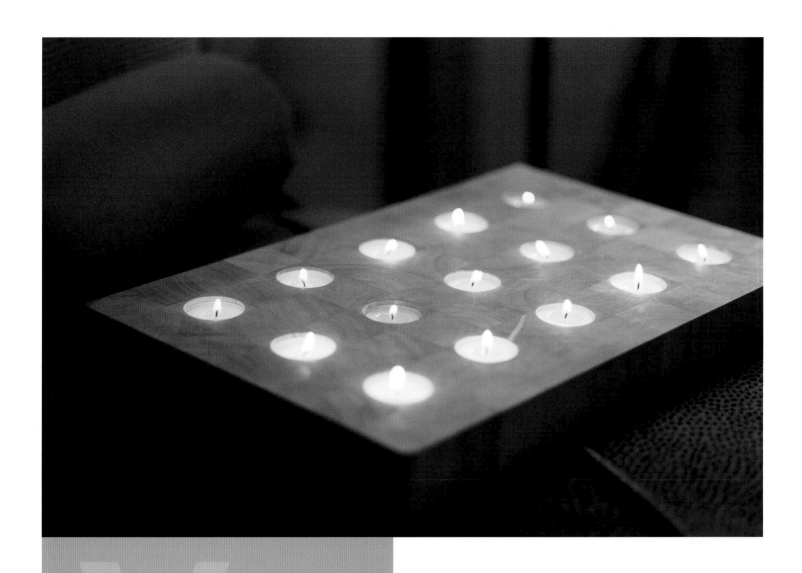

VARIATION

Another romantic glow can easily be created by drilling holes slightly deeper than the height of a tea-light candle into a wooden butcher-block cutting board.

BOOKCASE COVER

CASE CLOSED!

In our "before" of the room, the old bookcases were sturdy enough but just didn't fit our vision. Covering them in the same herringbone tweed as the bed cover, trimmed in the headboard's beige cotton, pulled it all together. Their front inverted pleats make for easy access into the shelves while keeping clutter out of view. We positioned the pair under two of our mirror-candle ledges and separated them with two silver-leaf–framed modern prints. The symmetry of the wall gives balance to the room and is aesthetically pleasing.

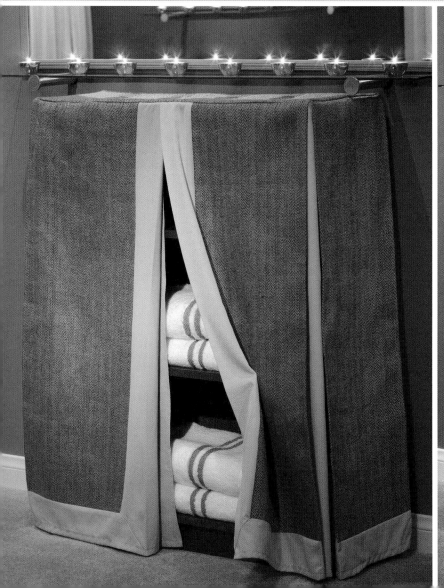

1 Measure the top, sides, front, and back of the bookcase. Add 5/8 inch to these for seam allowances. Cut one piece of fabric for the top, two for the sides, and one for the back. Measure the front, then cut two pieces plus seam allowance. For total coverage, you might want to overlap the front two pieces. If you decide to do this, add 1 inch to the width of each piece.

• Sew together the back, sides, and front pieces.

• Finish the edges of the front openings by turning them under 1/4 inch and stitching. Now join the strip of pieces (back, sides, and front) to the top piece, making sure to match the corners. Hem all around.

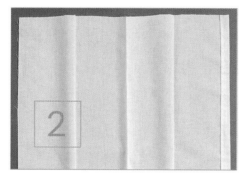

2 For a more designer look, add a 3-inch contrasting fabric border around the bottom and sew an inverted pleat for the opening. To create the inverted pleat:

• Determine the depth of the pleat. Say you want a 3-inch pleat. Quadruple the measurement, seam allowance (1 inch), and overlap allowance (1/2 inch). So, your measurement would be 13 1/2 inches.

• Cut the fabric into two panels and finish the opening side edges by turning under 1/4 inch and sewing.

3 Fold the panel accordion style to create a 3-inch pleat, and stitch along the top.

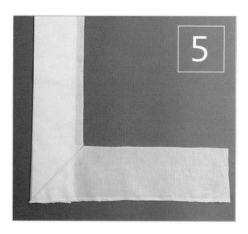

4 Repeat for the other side.

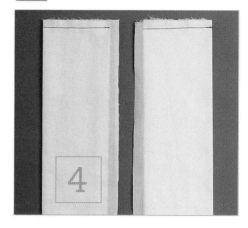

5 If desired, add mitered corners to the fabric border. Remember that? If not, check out pages 46–47).

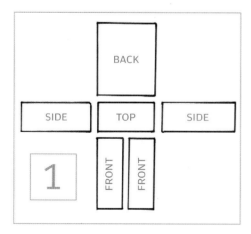

SYMMETRY

While I tend to favor a more asymmetrical design in other areas of the home, I prefer symmetry in the bedroom, with matching bed stands and lamps. I think it helps create the kind of harmony bedrooms should have.

Perfect symmetry against rich wall color gives power to inexpensive imported items. They amply fill the wall, making the carved chest appear larger than it really is.

Furniture placement can bring symmetry to any room. Here a left and right settee help define the conversation area.

Architectural embellishment, lighting, accessories, and furniture all work in consort to make a blank wall a room's focal point.

Carpet-diem

To add interest underfoot, we layered two area rugs on top of the existing wall-to-wall carpet. The larger, bottom rug, which was already in the room, acts as a border under the smaller top carpet. It echoes the geometric of the club chairs but on a larger scale.

Tin Type

For an inexpensive but effective side table, we went to a nursery and found this tin planter in a dark lead-gray to match the throw pillow and cover on the bed. To add a touch of greenery, we filled it with floral moss and topped it with a piece of beveled glass. Add a classic silver lamp, and the tableau is complete.

ADAPTATION:
FROM THEM TO HER

Okay, by now you know that by changing the fabrics and adding a new window treatment, you can transform a room. But do you ever get tired of seeing the different looks? Me neither. Here a traditional toile was paired with a small pinstripe. Isn't it amazing how that transforms a room?

Patterns, like this one from Simplicity, make sewing a breeze.

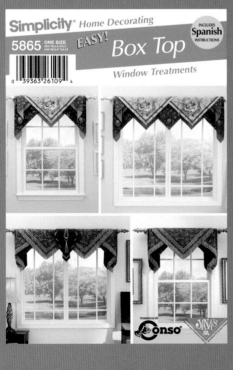

Simplicity® Home Decorating

5865 ONE SIZE UNA TALLA SOLA UNE SEULE TAILLE

EASY! **Box Top**

Window Treatments

INCLUDES **Spanish** INSTRUCTIONS

0 39363 26109 4

TRIMMINGS BY **Conso**®

Look how the bed takes on a different attitude if we just switch out the pillows.

SPACE: THE FINAL FRONT HALL

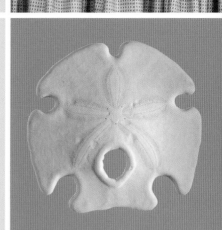

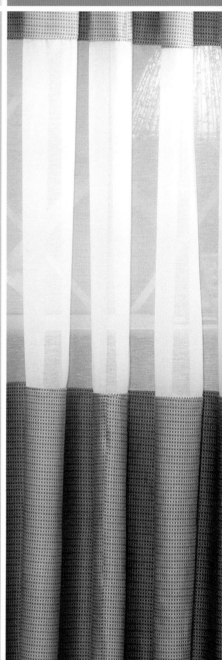

The entry hall is definitely one of the top-ten design challenges. People are always telling me that their entry halls stump them and that they consider these areas nothing more than pass-through spaces. They wonder what to do in them that won't impede the flow of traffic. Well, first of all, we're not auto-mobiles that require thoroughfares. Nor do we often have call for in-home square dancing halls or bowling alleys. So why shouldn't these vast corridors of empty space become pro-ductive areas of your home? Let's banish foyer fright forever, shall we?

The entry hall we tackled looked like those in many houses I've walked through, where a feeble attempt has been made to furnish the space with a narrow table and maybe a chair or two. Windowless hallways tend to frighten folks from using strong color. And while there might not be a lot of floor space, there is usually a ton of overhead space that goes unused—wasted space. Hate that! And hey, we're talking the first place your guests see when they come to visit, right? So let's make it count!

The fact is, beautiful wall color, great lighting, accessories, and, yes, even furniture can really bring these hallway areas alive. If the principles of those elements work in other areas of the home, why not in the entry, where the first impression is made?

Here a bookcase looks underwhelming in a back hall leading to the family room and kitchen. If, indeed, the idea is to decorate this area, perhaps wall-to-wall shelves displaying beautiful and interesting objects and art would be a nice solution. And the horizontal lines would help to pull the eye around the room. Another bookshelf is placed in an alcove opposite the stairs, taking up valuable wall space, while the center of the room remains empty. Hello?

Artwork seems underscaled for the height of the hall. And while the area is clean and tidy, it is certainly not what you'd call decorated. All that's about to change. Our goal is to not only employ my seven layers of design but also to create a functional, productive space.

Off the bat, I could easily see creating an art gallery effect on one wall, with a bit of a library, a work space, and even an upholstered bench for a touch of practical elegance. Focused, decorative lighting; properly scaled furniture; fabric; and most of all COLOR . . . will transform this I've-fallen-asleep-and-I-can't-wake-up space.

BEFORE

1 ATTITUDE

A clean and fresh combination of contrasting and organic materials evokes the spirit of ocean isles.

2 COLOR PALETTE

Blond woods and layered wovens contrast with a Greek island–inspired blue-green. The white trim becomes the bridge between the deep wall color and the rest of the room's blond elements, including nifty gallery railings that will be cut and fitted into our bookcases. A petite-check fabric with sheer insets will hide a center workstation when it is not in use.

3 TEXTURE

Rattan-covered ottomans, padded screens in grass cloth, and picture frames backed in reed matting all become the organic texture that keeps the space in its natural element.

4 ORGANIC ELEMENTS

Glass jars full of seashells and even a birdseed-encrusted entry-hall table will continue the layering process while reinforcing the seashore theme.

5 ACCENTS

The multiple sand dollars in the gallery area will set the precedent for white as an accent throughout the space. Whitewashed platters, white china, and coral sprays will become the final-touch accessories.

SMOOTH SAILING: A PORT IN THE CLUTTER STORM

As you first glance at what was basically a pass-through space, keep in mind what I always say: "If you can't build out, build up." And in this case I would add to that, "Build wall to wall to maximize every inch." The trick here is how to arrange and display, using closed containers for what you don't want to see and clear containers and open shelves for what you want to show off.

We used blue-green for our walls and painted the trim a fresh white. While the paint dried, we went shopping for more ready-to-assemble bookshelves that we could work a little decorative magic on to create a storage and office unit. We chose a wood laminate for the bookcases to match the stair and railing woods as closely as possible.

We placed one bookcase to the right of the back hall entrance, and placed two back-to-back across from the stairs. From one side of the back-to-back unit we built a bench, and from the other, a desk.

Then we wanted to play up the nautical theme we envisioned. In the Van Dyke's Restorers catalog we

Here is another great example of how mastering a few designer techniques can save you a lot of money and give you a big look.

Measure, cut, and glue—it's really that easy!

found what is called gallery railing, which comes in 6-foot lengths. This would be the perfect add-on to our plain-Jane bookcases. We cut the gallery rail to fit into the center shelves of each bookcase and on top, creating cornices. By attaching more gallery railing to the walls, we visually continued the line throughout the space for a great custom look.

Something to Rail Against

Gallery railing on both the bookcase shelves and on the wall as a chair rail creates a continual visual line that pulls several unrelated pieces together to look built in.

For the hall bench, we purchased a ready-to-assemble "Lack" unit from Ikea. The unit was turned sideways and a piece of foam was cut and slipcovered for a cushion (see page 142).

Above the bench we displayed a collection of framed sand dollars to emphasize the seashore theme (this is demonstrated on page 144).

For the desk, we cut a piece of medium-density fiberboard to fit into the bookcases that face each other. We chose to keep the surface wide enough for ample work space but narrow enough to allow a chair to be pulled up to it that would still be concealed when the unit's curtains were closed. The world does not need to see our messy desk, now, does it? Or, heaven forbid, the Visa bill, the novel in progress, or the steamy e-mails.

We hung a group of mirrors on the stairwell wall to reflect the shell gallery wall opposite. A ready-to-assemble table became the base to which we added glue, birdseed, and a glass top. This added an organic texture with a touch of whimsy. It's amazing what you can make for little money with a lot of imagination. We made the lamp with a lamp kit, a finial, a wooden plaque, and three wooden balls. Add a simple white shade and you're ready to come aboard, mate.

Now the back hall was wide enough for four floating shelves that would intrude only a foot into the space. But by installing shelves wall to wall and almost floor to ceiling, look at how much display and storage area we've created. This wall of shelves not only adds drama upon entering, but it also draws back the eye, adding beauty and depth to what was once just another pass-through space.

By establishing a theme and using one simple motif—in our case seashells—to pull it together, you really can create visual harmony in what might otherwise be open-shelf mayhem. If you keep to a low-key or neutral color palette, and focus on texture rather than pattern, you can accommodate lots of storage without sacrificing design.

"EEZY" BENCH CUSHION

SEWING LESSON

1 Cut 8-inch-thick foam to fit the seat.

2 Take the top measurement plus $\frac{1}{2}$ the depth of the cushion foam plus a $\frac{5}{8}$-inch seam allowance and cut two pieces of fabric. For example, if your foam piece is 20 inches by 20 inches by 4 inches, you will need two pieces of fabric measuring $22\frac{5}{8}$ by $22\frac{5}{8}$.

3 Using an iron, press the corners flat and stitch at the foam depth measurement. Fold out and press. Insert the foam and sew up.

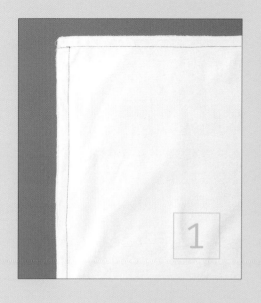

1

2

3

BEACHCOMBER'S CORNER: FRAMING NATURE

Framed original art is expensive. If you learn to make it yourself, you can adorn your walls while furthering the theme of a room and telling a great story. Our shell gallery arranged as a collection does the trick of bringing a bit of the beach to a humdrum pass-through space.

This project, including shopping, should take just a few hours.

MATERIALS AND TOOLS

Inexpensive unfinished frames

Paintbrushes

Base-color paint

Crackle medium or top-color paint (optional)

Scissors or an X-acto knife

Matting, caning, textured paper, or wallpaper

Spray adhesive

Hot-glue gun and glue sticks

Sand dollars or shells

1 Remove the backs from the frames and set them aside.

2 Paint the frames with a solid color or stain, or do a crackle finish as we did, following the instructions in the crackle-finish painting kit.

3 Using the cardboard insert in the frame as a template, cut new matting as a backdrop for the sand dollars. We use caning in this example, but other options include textured paper from an art store, wallpaper remnants, grass cloth, or even glazed paper bags—anything to add texture without overpowering the subject.

With spray-mount adhesive, glue the new mats to the existing picture backs. Once the backs are dry, reinsert them into the frames.

Hot-glue sand dollars or shells to the center of each frame.

HOW TO CREATE A CRACKLE FINISH

BASE COAT

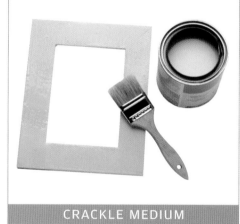

CRACKLE MEDIUM

TOP COAT

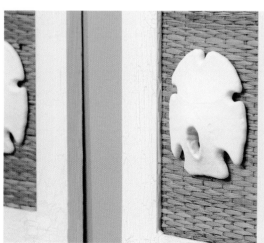

YOUR FIVE-YEAR-OLD CAN DO THIS

Color, texture, and theme create the perfect gallery wall for our Shore-inspired room.

Remember, a collection is three or more related pieces, from those little spoons you collected on your vacations to the leaves you picked up on an evening walk with the family. Featuring them in groups makes an interesting creative statement without saying "clutter."

Basket Case Solved

We arranged the floating back-hall shelves with an eye to symmetry. Baskets, trays, and shell-filled glass containers provide open and closed storage.

Grouping by Color

One of the tricks of merchandising is to arrange items by color. This allows you to bring together unrelated items in a harmonious still life. Our mix of odd serving pieces and seashells creates a curio-cabinet effect in a simple bookcase. While you are arranging, stand back every now and then and squint at your work in progress to make sure the items are balanced visually. It is also good to vary heights and shapes.

Power in Numbers

Here's a great way to showcase a collection that becomes the key element to the room's overall theme. One element used en masse creates a deliberate and poetic effect in what was once a plain-Jane bookcase. There is power in numbers.

Vase-ic Instinct

These sexy vases from a company called Umbra are cool on their own, but clustered together on top of a bookcase against rich wall color—WOW! Instant drama.

HIDING THAT
SEAM-Y SIDE

We used caning to cover the
same type of artists' canvas
stretchers used in our Loft room
and attached them to the sides of
the back-to-back bookcases to
hide the seam between them.
They also add visual softness to
the space.

CONTRAST CURTAIN

Curtains create privacy and hide clutter. This project is really nothing more than a shower rod and ready-made curtains that we jazzed up with a contrasting fabric panel sewn in. The bowed rod and extensions (if needed) are available at bed and bath stores.

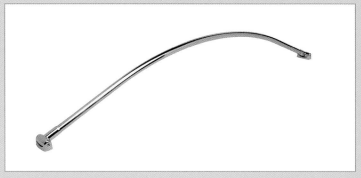

1 Determine the length of your curtain and divide by three. Add 1 inch of seam allowance to this measurement for the center fabric piece and the bottom fabric piece. Add 3 inches to this measurement when cutting the top piece to allow for a rod pocket. In our case, the bookcase was 78 inches tall, so the center and bottom panels were 26 inches, plus 1 inch for seam allowance. The top piece was 29 inches (the seam allowance has already been factored into this measurement).

For the top piece, turn the solid fabric down 1½ inches and stitch. Trim the excess. This is your rod pocket. The seam is on the backside.

2 Combine the top solid fabric with the sheer center fabric by stitching together their right sides. Trim the seam and press it with an iron.

3 Reinforce the seam with another row of stitching on the right side, about ¹/₄ inch from the first seam.

4 Repeat step 3 using the center and the bottom to connect them.

VARIATION
BORDER PATROL: FROM STORE-BOUGHT TO CUSTOM

Have you ever found that perfect drapery panel but it was too short? Me too. We paired this panel with a remnant we had from a previous project and added it to the bottom. Presto!
A totally custom panel.

HIDEAWAY DESK: A TWO-BOOKCASE STUDY

Out-of-the-way workstations for today's busy, online households can greatly improve our home's functionality. Here's an easy project that adapts ready-to-assemble bookcases from an office supply store to create a desk.

This project, including shopping, should take a full day.

MATERIALS AND TOOLS

Bookcases

Tape measure

Sheet of ³⁄₄-inch-thick medium-density fiberboard (MDF)

Jigsaw

³⁄₄-inch-thick half-round trim

Finishing nails

Hammer

Spackle

Primer

Paint roller

Paint

1-by-3-inch board the length of the desktop

Wood screws

Wall anchors

Drill

Fine-grit sandpaper

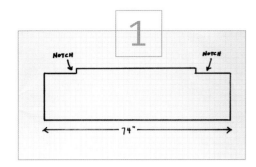

1

NOTCH   NOTCH

← 74" →

1 Determine where you want to place the bookcases. Once they are in place and facing each other, measure the distance between them and cut a piece of MDF for the desktop. In this example, the top measures 74 inches (from the back up each bookcase) by 24 inches. The 24-inch depth allows a chair to be pulled up to the desk and hidden behind a curtain attached to the bookcases as we have here.

2 If you want the desktop to fit flush against a long wall, you'll need to notch out both sides of your desktop to accommodate the depth of the bookcase sides that are against the wall. If you would rather leave that bit of space for electrical cords to drop behind, then do so. Another solution for dealing with cords is to cut a small hole in the desk surface to slip your phone and computer cords down unnoticed.

2

To finish the top, add a piece of ³/₄-inch half-round trim to the front edge of the desktop using finishing nails. Spackle, prime, and paint.

3 Adjust the bookcase shelves to your liking, one being at a good working height, on which your new desktop will rest.

Measure the distance between the fronts of the bookcases. Using this measurement, cut a 1-inch-thick by 3-inch-wide strip of wood to that length. This is a support to keep the desktop from bowing. Measure from the floor to what will be the bottom of the desk, and secure your support strip to the wall at that height. Make

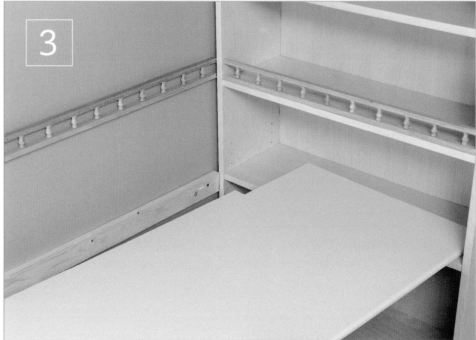

3

sure to screw into the studs. If there aren't any, use mollies to anchor the screws.

4 With the support strip secure, position the desktop on it, between the two bookcases. Secure the desktop to the support strip with wood screws from the top of the desk. Fill the screw holes with spackle and let dry. Sand smooth and touch up with paint.

4

The add-on gallery rail embellishes the shelf and continues at the same height along the wall. How cool is that?

IT'S ALL ABOUT TEXTURE

Adding texture rather than pattern makes a small space feel larger. Here the rib of the silk curtains, the texture of the bookcase panels, and the bleached-grass-cloth ottoman tell a story that is both chic and organic. Texture is timeless, while a print can be the first element to date a room.

V

VARIATION: TEXT-UR MESSAGE

Texture can be created on almost any surface. Using woven matting, rope, and bamboo strips, we transformed this mundane door. This same technique looks amazing on a ceiling.

MADE IN THE SHADE: SUPER-SIMPLE LAMP SHADE

Embellishing is a key component to customizing, and lamp shades are blank canvases for your creativity. Add wallpaper, trim, twine, tassels, or beads. Here we begin with a simple lamp shade, a skein of heavily textured yarn, and a ball of natural twine. The idea is to do a double wrap alternating the twine and the yarn for an interesting, textural effect.

This project, including shopping, should take just a few hours.

MATERIALS AND TOOLS

Skein of textured yarn

Lamp shade

Hot-glue gun and glue sticks

Spool of textured twine

1 Attach one end of the yarn to the inside of the shade with a dollop of hot glue. I like to start and end at the top inside. This way the beginning and end are together and the shade can be adjusted so that part is out of sight. Continue by wrapping the yarn vertically around the shade, leaving space for wrapping the twine in between.

2 In the spaces between the yarn, wrap the twine in the same direction. Remember to glue the end to the inside of the shade.

Such a simple idea, but you won't find another like it anywhere!

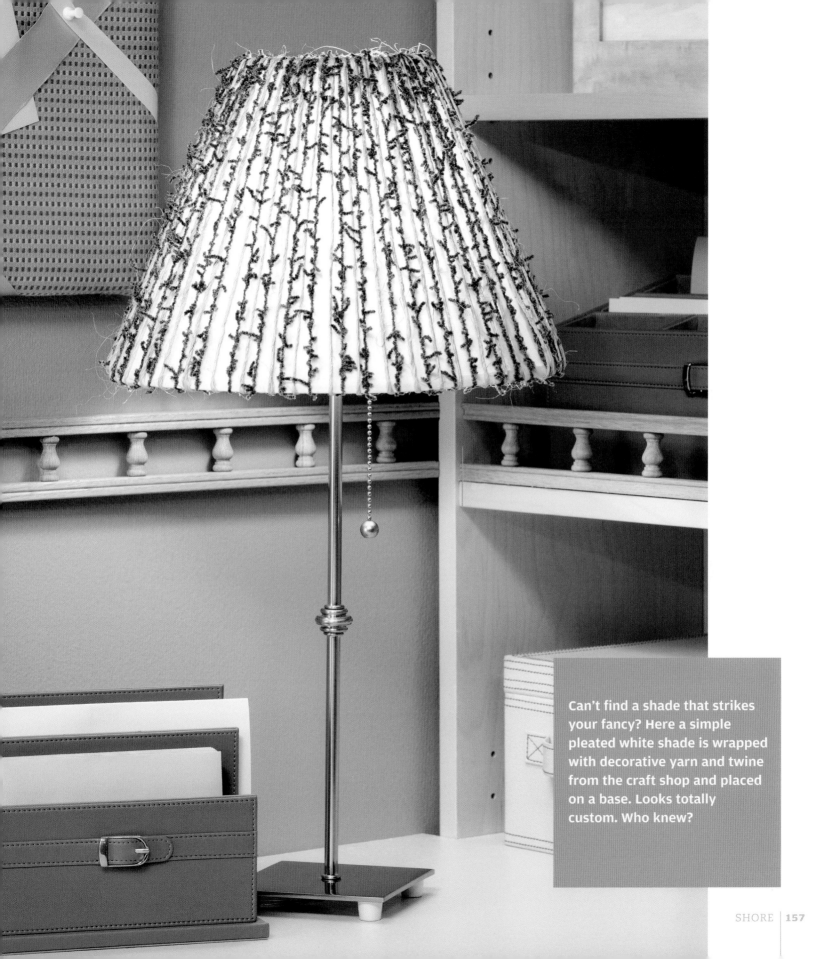

Can't find a shade that strikes your fancy? Here a simple pleated white shade is wrapped with decorative yarn and twine from the craft shop and placed on a base. Looks totally custom. Who knew?

The Big Picture

Order, texture, and a monochromatic color scheme create atmosphere in what was once a sterile entry hall. The rest is all about decorating and power in numbers. The repeated use of one or two key elements makes organization a beautiful thing.

AFTER

Bird's-Eye View

Our birdseed-covered entry table, finial lamp, mirrors, and flowers create a fresh tableau—a still life that takes up a small footprint.

Gone to Seed

Working in about a square-foot section at a time, we coated a simple ready-to-assemble table with white (okay, you are making me write the "c" word) CRAFT glue (whew! I made it!) and a layer of birdseed. Just pour the seeds on top of the glue and press lightly. Continue the process until the table is covered fully. It's fun and easy, and the result is one of a kind. A piece of glass cut to size protects the table's top and adds even more panache to an otherwise nondescript piece of furniture. You might also try "seeding" a decorative box, a lamp base, or a picture frame

LIGHT THE WAY

How easy is this? Very simple-to-do lamp kits are available at craft and hardware stores. Here we drilled a hole in the center of a painted wooden finial so we could feed the electrical cord through it. We then glued four painted wooden balls to the bottom, added a shade, and plugged in the drama! With a little imagination and an electrical lamp kit, almost anything can be turned into a base for a lighting fixture that is one of a kind. Find a cool object that promotes the theme of your room and go for it. In our case, a carved acorn finial from Van Dyke's Restorers Catalog (see Contact Information) sparked our creativity as a springboard for our Shore hallway.

This project, including shopping, should take just a few hours, and supplies are available at most craft shops and hobby stores.

MATERIALS AND TOOLS

Lamp kit

Large wooden finial

5/8-inch drill bit

Drill

Hacksaw (optional)

Small wooden balls (from the craft store—can be glued or screwed)

Paintbrush

Base-color paint

Crackle medium

Top-color paint

1. First, study the directions that come with whatever electrical lamp kit you purchase. Everything from the plug and socket to the shade harp should be included. This will give you a good idea of how to adapt the object of your desire into a functioning lamp.

2. We began by using a 5/8-inch drill bit measuring 16 inches long to bore a hole down the center of the finial. Your drill bit length will vary depending on how long a bit you need to get through whatever you are using as your base.

3. To accommodate our lamp kit's socket, we needed a flat surface. So with a saw, we lopped off the top of our finial. Again, your kit will indicate how you have to adapt your base.

4. As another detail, if you like, add wooden balls for feet at the base of the finial.

5. From the craft store we purchased a crackle finish kit and followed the directions. Most kits tell you to apply a base coat first. This is the color that you'll see the least of through the cracks of the top coat. Once the base coat is dry, apply the clear crackle medium, and once that dries, the top coat (the color you'll see the most of). And the cracking happens all by itself—magic!

6. Finish wiring the base, if you haven't already.

7. Add a nice shade or embellish one like we've done on page 156.

OH, WHAT A RELIEF IT IS: EASY 3-D STENCILING

Stenciling is a marvelous way to add your own touch to everything, from a dresser front, to a decorative box, to a chair back ... well, you get the idea. This 3-D effect can actually simulate carved relief on almost anything. Applied at the top of a wall near the ceiling, it can give a great, carved-plaster effect. Use these details sparingly and they'll remain special additions to any environment.

For this project, we took advantage of the French-inspired tin containers that are in abundance in most craft stores. But we wanted them to actually look like French flea-market finds.

Including shopping, this project should take about half a day total; though it does require a step to dry overnight.

MATERIALS AND TOOLS

Metal container

Primer

2 paintbrushes, one for container surface and one smaller, stiffer one for stencil

Base-color paint

Removable spray adhesive

Plastic stencil

Flexall

Paint tint

Spackle knife or stiff paintbrush

Glaze, tinted brown (optional)

Rag

1 Prime a plain metal container. (Products like Rust-Oleum, BIN, or Kilz work well on nonporous surfaces and some are available in spray cans to make priming even easier.)

Once the primer is dry, apply a base coat of paint. Since this was going into our Shore room, we used a cream color.

2 It's time to stencil. Spray a thin mist of removable spray adhesive to coat the back of the stencil. This will allow it to stick to the container without moving.

3 Rather than a plain, flat painted stencil, we wanted more of a 3-D-relief effect. For that, we used a patching compound called Flexall, which comes premixed in a tub. We mixed paint tint, which was purchased at a super-hardware store, to color the compound.

Using a spackle knife or a stiff brush for a thicker relief effect, apply the tinted compound to the area left open by the stencil.

Remove the stencil while the compound is still pliable and let the tin dry overnight.

4 For an antiqued effect, apply a translucent brown paint glaze over the entire container and selectively dab off some of the glaze with a soft paint rag. This filled in the nooks and crannies for the aged effect we desired.

ADAPTATION: MAP QUESTING

PRESTO-CHANGE-O

Using these materials and patterns, our friends at Jo-Ann Stores redid the desk area to show you that with a simple change of fabric and accessories, you can achieve an entirely different look.
I am "Shore" you can do it!

Simplicity *Home Decorating*
5121 simply✳teen
Easy Window Treatments

0 39363 27585 5

Simplicity *Home Decorating*
4529 simply✳teen
Organizers

0 39363 29183 1

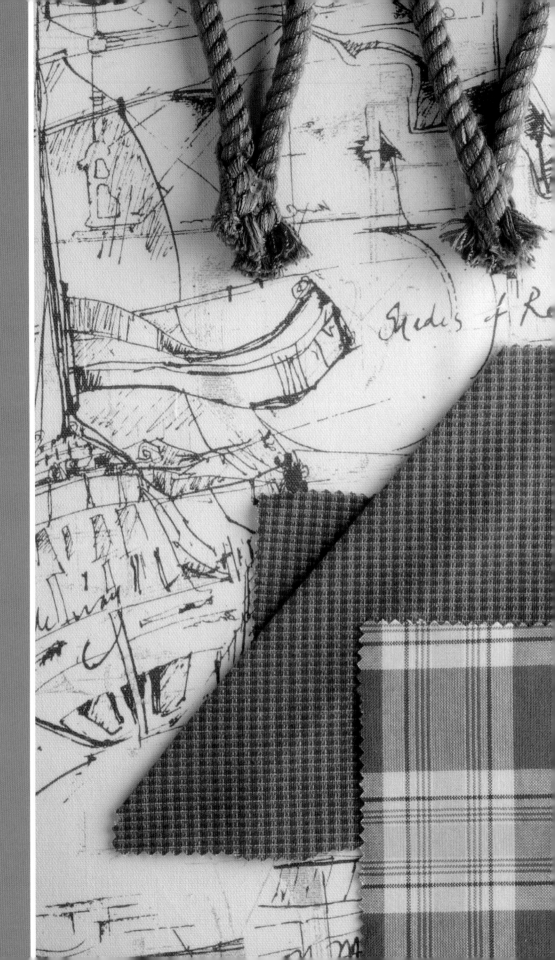

CONCLUSION

So here I am with my crew, crossing the last t's, dotting the missed i's, giving this book its final polish. We've tried hard to make sure the ideas we've presented are ready for you to implement. Frankly, some of our ideas didn't make the cut. While some projects were easy, the time commitment was too great. And today it is the lack of time even more than the lack of money that seems to rob us of the quality of life that we all deserve. We've gone from tasking to multitasking to megatasking. I wish I could say I see a slowdown coming soon, but I don't; it's simply part of our lives. That's one of the reasons it's important to make time to get it together at home. You should be blown away by how cool your space is every time you walk through the front door. What you see should inspire you, tell your story, and make you proud.

We've shared with you some of our best ideas—concepts that can be your launching point to making your home a true reflection of who you are. A little batting and fabric, the right wall color, and a simple rearranging of furniture can make all the difference. We've shown you how to update, disguise, embellish, and assemble using tools and materials readily available right near your own home. We've shown you how pass-through spaces can become functional and elegant. Just to prove that size is irrelevant, we've tackled single rooms that have to function in a variety of ways. We've shown you how to marbleize old kitchen counters you thought you'd be stuck with. We've shown you how to make ordinary, inexpensive bookcases into room dividers, extra seating, and workstations. We put windows where there weren't any, and we made a beautiful bedroom from simple hollow-core doors and cinder blocks—who knew, right?

So what are you waiting for? It's not because you can't do the projects, because most of them are simple. And it's not about the time, because almost all of the projects take less than a day to do. (Sometimes we have to let paint dry overnight.) If you're feeling insecure because you've never done anything like this before, that's okay; you're only human. But don't let that get in your way and don't be afraid—those fears can suck the life out of the room and with it the most important thing you bring to the table: your creativity. No one says you have to be talented, but to deny your inherent personal creativity is silly. Remember when you first sat at a computer and felt like a dunce? Now it's a part of your everyday life. You're surfing the Net, text messaging, and e-mailing from anywhere at anytime. If you can do that, you're *over*qualified to do the projects in this book.

Think about it. We have a chance today to live any way we want to. We have resources that our parents never imagined. We can shop online in our jammies, take photos with our telephones, and pay four bucks for a nonfat latte with low foam. We've come a long way, baby. The point is, no one will chastise you for not having a formal living room or a dining room that seats twelve. Our lives have changed, and so must our homes as we prepare for the future.

So give yourself permission to learn something new that could change your attitude about who you are. As hard as you work, your home should be an antidote to stress—your haven in which to nest and recharge.

We know how hard change is and how easy it is to get used to things remaining the same. But we also know how transforming change can be. We've read thousands of your letters telling us that once you began the process of change in your homes, you felt a rekindled creative spirit you didn't think you had. That's powerful. It's happened to thousands of our readers and viewers, and it can happen to you!

You can do it!

RESOURCES

Our resource guide has been organized by room and according to my Seven Layers of Design.

TOWN: LOFTY IDEAS

Paint
Christopher Lowell Designer Paint
Walls: Walnut Shell
Trim: Arrowroot

Molding, ceiling medallions
Focal Point Architectural Products

Ceiling tiles
M-Boss

Sofa, sofa table, ottoman
Flexsteel/Christopher Lowell Home Collection

Desk chairs, accessories
Office Depot/Christopher Lowell Office Collection

Fabric, canvas stretchers
Jo-Ann Stores

Woven blinds
3 Day Blinds/Christopher Lowell Collection

Bookcases
Sauder

Cubes, dressers
IKEA

Storage boxes, magazine holders, accessories
The Container Store

Picture frames, RAKA "X" table, lamps, towel bars, accessories
Umbra

No-Kord Picture Lights
Hobby Hill Lighting

Plants/trees
Trees International

Patterns: adaptation
Simplicity

COUNTRY:
OPEN TO THE PUBLIC:
SHARED SPACES

Paint
Christopher Lowell Designer Paint
Walls: Creamed Asparagus and Clay Cotta
Trim: Peas and Cream
Accent used in marbleizing: Arrowroot

Media-center armoire
Office Depot/Christopher Lowell Office Collection

Sectional, coffee table
Flexsteel/Christopher Lowell Home Collection

Fabric, canvas stretchers
Jo-Ann Stores

"Lack" units
IKEA

Slide coat hook, cabinet drawer pulls, accessories
Umbra

Unfinished picture frames, wood drawer, nail-head trim kit
Jo-Ann Stores

Patterns: adaptation
Simplicity

CITY: SEXY SPACES:
MASTERING THE MASTER

Paint
Christopher Lowell Designer Paint
Walls: Dried Blueberry
Accent used on cornices: Navy Bean

Chairs
Flexsteel/Christopher Lowell Home Collection

Fabric
Jo-Ann Stores

Area rugs
IKEA

Clocks
Umbra

Bamboo
Loose Ends

No-Kord Picture Light
Hobby Hill Lighting

Patterns: adaptation
Simplicity

SHORE SPACE:
THE FINAL FRONT HALL

Paint
Christopher Lowell Designer Paint
Walls: White Pepper
Trim: White

Gallery railing, wood acorn
Van Dyke's Restorers

Chairs, desk accessories
Office Depot/Christopher Lowell Office Collection

Fabric, lamp shades, and picture frames
Jo-Ann Stores

"Lack" units, bookcases, floating shelves
IKEA

Ottoman, storage containers, glass jars
The Container Store

Woven matting/caning
Loose Ends

Mirrors, accessories
Umbra

Flexall
Custom Building Products

Patterns: adaptation
Simplicity

CONTACT INFORMATION

Christopher Lowell Designer Paint
866-362-7559
www.christopherlowell.com

The Container Store
888-CONTAIN (266-8246)
www.containerstore.com

Custom Building Products
800-272-8786
www.custombuildingproducts.com

Flexsteel/Christopher Lowell Home Collection
800-685-7632
www.flexsteel.com

Focal Point Architectural Products
800-662-5550
www.focalpointap.com

Hobby Hill Lighting
866-PIC-LITE (742-5483)
www.hobbyhill.com

IKEA
800-434-IKEA (4532)
www.ikea.com

Jo-Ann Stores
800-739-4120
www.joann.com

Loose Ends
866-390-2348
www.looseends.com

M-Boss
866-88MBOSS (886-2677)
www.mbossinc.com

Office Depot/Christopher Lowell Office Collection
800-463-3768
www.officedepot.com

Sauder
800-523-3987
www.sauder.com

Simplicity
888-588-2700
www.simplicity.com

3 Day Blinds/Christopher Lowell Collection
800-800-3329
www.3day.com

Trees International
888-873-3799
www.treesinternational.com

Umbra
800-387-5122
www.umbra.com

Van Dyke's Restorers
800-558-1234
www.vandykes.com

ACKNOWLEDGMENTS

Writing instructional, photo-laden books is no small task. It takes a lot of dedicated people to make sure my books are truly meaningful to you. So this page gives me the chance to thank the many people whom you might not otherwise hear of—all working in consort to ensure that the next addition to the Christopher Lowell library is of the highest quality. So, here it goes. Thank you to Frances Schultz, who edits my books, making the content clear while preserving my voice— keeping it ever-present. I'd like to thank my staff here at Christopher Lowell Enterprises: Michael Murphy and Jocelyne Borys, my creative team, along with construction foreman, Adam Kahn, for caring about every little detail and helping me bring the vision of this book alive. Thanks to our photography crew, Scott Dunbar and Rich Wysockey, and our contributing photographer, Douglas Hill. Thanks to Daniel Levin, my COO and manager, for his contributions to my business and to me. Thanks to Todd Optican, of Marketing, for coordinating the various partners who have made their contributions, especially the staff of Jo-Ann Stores, spearheaded by Tim Riggle and Rachel Wright with Eva Orleans, Valerie Miranda, and Carmen Ortega. A special thanks to Sohayla Cude, who keeps the information flowing between everyone. Thank you to my financial team, Gerri Leonard and her staff, including our daily point person, Shelly Gates. In our Communications Department, thanks to Janet Newell and my sister Laura McBride. Also thanks to Kelly Johnston and Jacqueline Johnson for keeping the home fires stoked. At Clarkson Potter Publishers, a special thanks to Lauren Shakely, and to Aliza Fogelson, Maggie Hinders, Doris Cooper, Tammy Blake, and Amy Corley. And lastly, thanks to our valued readers who allow us to inspire, motivate, and help make your home a true reflection of who you are.

INDEX

A

Accent elements
  entry hall, 135
  kitchen/family room,
    65
  master bedroom, 99
  studio apartment, 25
Accessories
  accent pillows, 76, 77,
    116–17, 129
  choosing, tips for, 50
  grouping by color, 147
  grouping by numbers,
    148
  inexpensive ideas for,
    39
Apartment makeover,
    2–59
Artwork, 132
Attitude, creating
  entry hall, 135
  kitchen/family room,
    65
  master bedroom, 99

B

Bamboo vases, 118–19
Banquette seating
  constructing, 71–72
  sewing cushion cover
    for, 74
Baskets, 141
Bed linens

buying, 95, 97
  fabrics, 58–59
  mitered corner duvet,
    46–47
  trends in, 117
Bedroom. *See also* Bed
  linens; Beds
  creating symmetry in,
    124–25
  master bedroom
    makeover, 94–129
Beds
  bookcase headboard,
    27–28, 44–45
  in one-room living
    space, 22, 26
  padded headboard,
    110–12
  platform bed, 113–15
Benches
  banquette cushion
    cover, 74
  banquette-style, 71–72
  creating cushion for,
    140, 142–43
  made with ottomans,
    52–54
Birdseed-covered table,
    159
Bolster-backed ban-
    quette, 71–72
Bolster window toppers,
    73

Bookcases
  adding gallery railing
    to, 140
  creating bed surround
    with, 27–28, 44–45
  creating desk with,
    152–53
  creating fabric curtain
    for, 122–23
  for entry hall, 132, 137
  lining with mirrors, 56
  open and closed stor-
    age in, 141, 147
  separating living
    spaces with, 22, 26
  side-by-side, hiding
    seam, 149
  sides of, displaying
    items on, 40
Bureau dresser drawers,
    55

C

Cabinets, kitchen, 63, 67
Cactus garden, 38
Candle ledges, 120–21
Carpeting, 126
Ceiling, adding texture
    to, 155
Chair rail, 140
Chairs
  club, for bedroom, 101
  dining room, 62, 82

City lifestyle
  decorating style, 15, 17
  master bedroom
    makeover, 94–129
Clutter, 22, 122, 151
Coffeemakers, 51
Coffee table, 36–37
Color palettes
  bedroom, 99
  entry hall, 135
  kitchen/family room,
    65
  studio apartment, 25
Contrast curtain, 150–51
Cornices, window, 104,
    106–8
Countertop, faux marble,
    67, 78–81
Country lifestyle
  decorating style, 15, 17
  kitchen/family room
    makeover, 60–93
Creativity command-
    ments, 18–19
Curtain, contrast, 150–51
Cushion, for bench,
    142–43

D

Decorative accessories
  accent pillows, 76,
    116–17, 129
  choosing, tips for, 50

grouping by color, 147
grouping by numbers,
148
inexpensive ideas for,
39
Desks
for entry hall, 140,
152–53
fabrics for, 164–65
for studio apartment,
30–31
Dining room chairs,
62
Dining room table,
painting, 82–84
Drapery panels, 151
Dressers
bedside, 101
drawer makeover, 55
Duvet, mitered corners
for, 46–47

E
Entry hall makeover,
130–65

F
Fabrics
for bed linens, 58–59
for desk workstations,
164–65
faux poodle fur, 109,
116–17
floating fabric panel,
48–49
transforming room
with, 128–29
upholstery, choosing,
76
Faux marble countertop,
67, 78–81

Faux poodle fur lamp
shades, 109
Faux poodle fur pillow,
116–17
Floating fabric panel,
48–49
Framed seashells, 144–45
Furniture placement
for conversation area,
125
sketching out, 26

G
Gallery railing, 140

H
Hallway makeover,
130–65
Headboard projects
made with bookcases,
27–28, 44–45
padded headboard,
110–12

K
Kitchen cabinets, 63, 67
Kitchen countertops, 67,
78–81
Kitchen/family room
makeover, 60–93

L
Lamps
country-chic, 88–89
faux poodle fur–
covered shades, 109
finial, 141, 160–61
hanging, customizing,
92–93
textured shades,
156–57

Lighting. See also Lamps
mood lighting, 101,
104
rope lighting, 104
Linens, bed
buying, 95, 97
fabrics, 58–59
mitered corner duvet,
46–47
trends in, 117

M
Marbleizing, with paint,
78–81
Mirrors
attaching to storage
tower, 35
as candle ledges, 120
for creating illusion of
space, 28
framed, hanging on
wall, 32–33
hanging on stairwell
wall, 140
lining backs of shelves
with, 56
Mitered corners, for
duvet, 46–47

N
Nail head trim–edged
table, 87
Nightstands, 101,
113–15

O
Organic elements
entry hall, 135
master bedroom, 99
studio apartment, 25
Ottoman bench, 52–54

P
Paint
distressed, for dining
table, 82–84
faux marble, for coun-
tertop, 67, 78–81
Pillows, accent
for beds, 129
covering with faux
poodle fur, 116–17
sewing piping to edges,
77
for sofas, 76
Projects
adding mitered cor-
ners to duvet,
46–47
back-bolstered ban-
quette, 71–72
bamboo vases, 118–19
banquette cushion
cover, 74
bench cushion, 142–43
birdseed-covered entry
table, 159
bookcase-backed
headboard, 44–45
bookcase cover, 122–23
bureau dresser
makeover, 55
buying tools for, 19
candle ledges, 120–21
contrast curtain,
150–51
country-chic lamp,
88–89
covering bookcase
seams with caning,
149
creating a faux
window, 106–8

customizing lamp shades and cords, 92–93

distressed dining table, 82–84

entryway desk, 152–53

faux marble counter-top, 78–81

faux poodle fur lamp shades, 109

finial lamp, 160–61

floating fabric panels, 48–49

framed seashells, 144–45

hanging framed mir-rors on wall, 32–33

inexpensive decorative accessories, 39

lazy swivel storage unit, 34–35

nail head trim–edged table, 87

padded headboard, 110–12

pipe-dream coffee table, 36–37

piping edging, 77

platform bed, 113–15

raised panel walls, 86

resources for ideas, 58

rope-trimmed vases, 90–91

sand-sational cactus garden, 38

stenciled tin contain-ers, 162–63

studio apartment desk, 30–31

textured door, 155

textured lamp shade, 156–57

tin planter side table, 127

top ten creativity tips, 18–19

upholstered ottoman bench, 52–54

R

Railing, gallery, 140

Refrigerators, compact, 51

Rope lighting, 104

Rope-trimmed vases, 90–91

Rugs, 126

S

Sand dollars, 140

Seashells, framed, 144–45

Sewing lessons
adding mitered cor-ners to duvet, 46–47
banquette cushion cover, 74
bench cushion, 142–43
bookcase cover, 122–23
contrast curtain, 150–51
piping edging, 77

Shore lifestyle
decorating style, 15, 17
entry hall makeover, 130–65

Sofas
choosing fabrics for, 76
color of, 62
placement of, 125

Stenciled tin containers, 162–63

Storage
in bookshelves, 141, 147
closed storage, 28
open storage, 28
ottoman bench, 52–54

Storage tower, 34–35

Studio apartment makeover, 2–59

Symmetry, in bedroom, 124–25

T

Tables
bedside, 101, 113–15
birdseed-covered, 140–41, 159
coffee table, 36–37
dining room, painting, 82–84
nail head trim edging for, 87
side, made from tin planter, 127

Texture
entry hall, 135
kitchen/family room, 65
for making small space feel larger, 154
master bedroom, 99
studio apartment, 25
transforming door with, 155

Tin containers, stencil-ing, 162–63

Tools, 19

Town lifestyle
decorating style, 15, 17

studio apartment makeover, 2–59

TV storage tower, 34–35

U

Upholstered ottoman bench, 52–54

Upholstery fabrics, choosing, 76

V

Vases
bamboo, 118–19
decorating with, 148
rope-trimmed, creat-ing, 90–91

W

Walls
adding gallery railing to, 140
bedroom, colors for, 97, 100–101, 104
kitchen/family room, colors for, 67
nailing bead board sheets to, 67
raised paneling for, 86

Window cornices, 104, 106–8

Windows, "creating," 106–8

Window treatments
bolster toppers, 73
drapery panels, 151
"increasing" window size with, 62
new fabrics for, 128–29
sketching out, 26

Workstations, 30–31, 152–53